A DIVORCE LAWYER'S
GUIDE TO MARRIAGE

A DIVORCE LAWYER'S GUIDE TO MARRIAGE

William Hood

Book Guild Publishing
Sussex, England

First published in Great Britain in 2012 by
The Book Guild Ltd
Pavilion View
19 New Road
Brighton, BN1 1UF

Copyright © William Hood 2012

The right of William Hood to be identified as the author of
this work has been asserted by him in accordance with the
Copyright, Designs and Patents Act 1988.

All rights reserved. No part of this publication may be reproduced,
transmitted, or stored in a retrieval system, in any form or by any
means, without permission in writing from the publisher, nor be
otherwise circulated in any form of binding or cover other than
that in which it is published and without a similar condition being
imposed on the subsequent purchaser.

Typesetting in Garamond by
Keyboard Services, Luton, Bedfordshire

Printed and bound in Great Britain by
CPI Group (UK) Ltd, Croydon, CR0 4YY

A catalogue record for this book is available from
The British Library

ISBN 978 1 84624 694 4

*To my beloved wife Sheila, who has shown me the way.
She is my Queen upon our chessboard.*

With acknowledgement of the works of Barbara Wadsworth, a gifted therapist, and of Eugene Halliday, an artist of wisdom and truth.

Contents

Introduction		1
1	Appetite	5
2	Gender	13
3	Love	29
4	Children	37
5	Finances	51
6	Sex	59
7	Emotions	67
8	Opposition	75
9	Age Difference	83
10	Religion	89
11	Conclusions	97

Introduction

I was eighteen years old when I interviewed my first divorce client. Fresh from school, four months into my five-year legal training contract as they are now called. Those were the days before students' rights and minimum wages. A pound a week, which didn't even cover my train fare to the office, was about it. I was let loose on unsuspecting clients as soon as I was taught how to take a basic statement of evidence. The trick was to cover every conceivable aspect of a client's story and then a more experienced eye would do the editing. At a pound a week it didn't really matter how long you took and being thrown in at the deep end with clients had its advantages. If you made mistakes no one blamed you and I learned quickly how to relate to a client in interview.

My first solo interview was with Mrs Poutoir or more correctly Madame Poutoir. She was more than twice my age. I was to discover that her French husband beat her regularly for his perverse pleasure. He demanded sexual favours I had never heard of and seemed to control her life in every way.

I recall being heartbroken when 'Madame' revealed to me, blow by blow, the intimate details of her husband's cruel behaviour. She was beautiful. How could he do it and how could she let it happen? I could not understand why she was still with him. With hindsight I was too young to take the interview. I became determined to see Monsieur Poutoir pay for his matrimonial 'crimes'. He, however, defended his wife's petition to divorce him.

In 1963 defended divorces were conducted in open court, with the public able to attend, before a senior judge with each party giving oral evidence on oath. Rigorous cross examination was allowed even of the most fragile of wives.

The case was not easy. In those ancient days continued sexual relations by an offended spouse condoned the other's cruelty and wiped the slate clean for each morning after! However, our barrister argued that the perverse sex had become part of the cruelty. Mr Poutoir thought differently. He believed a wife must do her master's bidding and it was not the business of anyone else to interfere. A husband could not be guilty of raping his lawful wedded and 'bedded' wife. There could be no such cruelty in marriage. However, when a man like Mr Poutoir, indeed any man, believes his own sexual ego to be indestructible he is heading for trouble. And when his meek and mild wife grows teeth he is entering the jaws of marital doom. Men like Poutoir make a fatal mistake. They confuse passivity in a woman with weakness. Push a lady too far and her strength knows no bounds. Indeed it *is* boundless; for it is feminine power at work compared with the limited energy of the ego-bound man.

Madame Poutoir found the courage to tearfully describe her ordeals in dramatic detail to the judge whilst her perverted husband sat powerless to intervene.

So began my 'divorcing' career. A lawyer's stock in trade is people and their personal lives each tell a unique story.

INTRODUCTION

Despite modern ways of living most human beings need and seek a personal relationship with another and the search for that loving and caring partner has never been stronger. The newspaper advertisements, the dating websites, the lonely hearts clubs and the 'singles' venues and ventures all provide testimony to this fact.

Marriage remains the goal for many of us. Some say it is a line of least resistance and is outdated, but marriage still signifies security, affirmation to each other of 'specialness', a loving commitment and is a recognised institution in society. Nevertheless, marriage is on the decline due to a number of factors. Economics, keeping one's options open, the declining necessity of shotgun weddings, abortions sufficing if the baby is unwanted, a social acceptance of children outside wedlock and less religious dogma have all played a part in cutting the marriage rate. Yet, to marry the one you profess to love is a joyous achievement for many people and to give and receive each other in matrimony at every level of being in mind, soul and body remains a wonderful ideal.

Nevertheless, so many marriages end in divorce. Life does not stand still. People change and their needs change. Is that the reason for divorce? Our personal landscapes change so we move on to the next need requiring fulfilment? Or is it that our expectations are dashed to the ground by the harsh problems of living in our fast moving society, particularly in the material atmosphere of the Western world? Or is it to do with an ignorance of what marriage is truly about? Perhaps the doctrine of 'till death us do part' is waning as the young slowly break the shackles of outmoded moral doctrines imposed by generations of churchgoing dogma.

It is said that prevention is better than cure. When a

spouse is seeking divorce it is usually too late to 'save the marriage', whatever we might mean by such an emotive phrase. The only real chance we have of creating marital risk management is to have some real understanding of the basic qualities of our human nature. So when a person is deciding to marry they do so in a more enlightened way or, if already married, and when they encounter a marital problem, they handle it with more understanding than might otherwise be the case. I shall try in this short book to offer my 'penny's worth' of learning to both those of you intending to marry and those of you who have already taken the plunge in the hope that at least some morsels of its content ring a bell of truth.

There is no 'should', 'ought' or 'must' in this book. Each of us has a unique journey to make as we travel through life. Mistakes will be made and all of them are grist to the mill for our personal growth and self development. I have no wish to encourage avoidance of living life to the full, which surely includes being prepared to make mistakes as we go. My aim is to try and shed some light upon the marital path so the potholes along its way are more readily navigated. There is nothing new in this book. All has been said before but this is my way of saying it from a divorce lawyer's point of view. I believe it is helpful to acquire some understanding of the essential energies of human nature which, from times long ago, have influenced our personal relationships. Also, I intend to address some areas of marital life which at times may become problematic during a marriage.

1

Appetite

When mankind first trod the earth it was raw in tooth and claw. It was a time when appetite was primal, before we were moulded into our so-called civilised society. Most of us don't eat each other any more. It became uneconomic to have your tribal neighbour boiled or roasted for Sunday lunch. To fancy your beloved so much that you ate them proved self-defeating. The appetite for flesh had to be curtailed. Kissing and related oral activities, albeit somewhat ferocious in early times, grew to be a more economic expression of one's hunger for carnal satisfaction. Yet, love bites still appear in tender places! Since the beginning of mankind's appearance on earth appetite untamed has spelt trouble and for the most part we have learnt the hard way by experience. Particularly, when in our prime years, we may bite off more than we can chew. You may hear a lover say, 'Darling, I love you so much I could eat you.' It's a figure of speech of course, but the origins of the emotional state operating in such a lover go way back in the annals of time. Mothers say it about their adorable young children and indeed other mothers' children! The river of appetite for the flesh and its pleasures runs deep. Flesh desires flesh and the more appealing the better. If you have any doubt that this is the case then just look at the media hype and market products encouraging you to look good, sexy and desirable! There is only one flesh but many bodies of it. Basically, it is self-devouring.

So, for starters we have basic appetite. You cannot get rid of it. You may try to control it or deny it, inhibit it or refine it, but it will not go away. It will eat us up inside, never mind someone else, if we try to stultify it. Appetite is intrinsic to life force energy and is essential to living a happy and full life. Personal and intimate relationships start because of an appetite for one another or perhaps several different appetites as they combine to produce an irresistible cocktail for personal relationships. A healthy appetite for your beloved is a very important positive in your relationship. However, the pleasure we derive from gratifying appetite is primarily pleasure for us and does not alone equal a love or even a true caring for one's 'lover'. We tend to 'love' the pleasures derived from our loved one. We are 'in love' with the pleasures gained from our relationship, but we may not love our willing playmate at all. Take the pleasures away or wait until the appetite wanes, or changes, or is satiated and the relationship may struggle to find alternative pastures of meaning.

Therefore, it is a wise move to be as objective and truthful to yourself as you are able about the nature and extent of your appetite for your beloved and do your best to avoid emotional confusion. Do not confuse the emotional force of your appetite with a true love for your lover.

Alas, the difficulty for many people is they do not see or care about such a confusion and do not distinguish between appetite and love. They are hell bent on having their relationship anyway, which is understandable, but then they go and spoil it all by getting married. It is expected or hoped that all else will follow, such as enough money, children, houses, cars, holidays and happiness.

People marry for all sorts of motives and reasons and often are not aware of many of them at the time they marry. An appetite for a 'live-in' companion may be as strong as an appetite for good sex, yet neither spell love. Appetite is the spice of life but if not seen for what it is, much heartache can follow in its wake. We may put up with dislikes to get what we like. When the likes begin to fade or become habitual and no longer stimulating, the inhibited dislikes slowly emerge to undermine the relationship. A lack of caring, disinterest, complaints and a general malaise in the relationship may begin to surface and if the will to love is not there to overcome the obstacles they may gather force.

A young lady came to see me in tears because her three-year-old 'marriage' had come adrift. Jennifer was a very pretty, almost porcelain type, example of angelic loveliness.

'He just doesn't love me any more. He never comes near me and has no time for what I say,' she explained. She was heartbroken. 'He's started staying out late and I can't bear it. He loved me so much to begin with; he couldn't leave me alone. Where has it all gone?' she asked. 'I thought we were married forever.'

'It is hard to accept, Jennifer, but sometimes our feelings of so-called love are more to do with the pleasures derived from what our lover has to offer. There is no real love or at least no developed love actually operating. It is the image we make of each other and the pleasures we give each other that we passionately like to experience. But take the pleasures away, or wait for them to wane, or watch them turn tail into dislike with our manufactured image of our beloved crumbling before our eyes and we have a very different marital playing field.' Jennifer was not saying a word, but I had her attention so I continued. 'True love, Jennifer, is not based in the emotions of liking or disliking. Love is above both these emotional states and you and Colin will either make love work or your attempts at being married will fail. Making love work is a lot more than merely that loving feeling.'

The tears came again and droplets began to trickle down her pale white cheeks.

'He says my breasts have shrunk and they need to be larger. He used to love them and say how much they belonged to him and no one else must ever touch them. He said he loved my softness.'

'See what I mean?' I said.

'What do you mean?' she asked whilst plundering my tissue box.

'He says he loved your body, but actually he just liked very much the pleasure of you.'

'I don't want him any more,' she replied. 'It hurts too much. If he doesn't love me then I want him out of the house.'

'Do you mean you don't want him or don't love him?'

'He doesn't touch me any more. We haven't made love for months. He doesn't help in the house and he prefers his mates to me.'

'Jennifer, do you love him?'

She raised her embarrassed head. 'I'm not sure. I thought I did, but I don't know.'

We sat in silence for a few moments. Then she volunteered, 'You know, I'm not sure I know what love is.'

'You are not alone,' I said. 'But in marriage I do believe we have a chance of finding out. Usually it's trial and error with all sorts of mistakes along the way.'

'God!' she exclaimed. 'You mean we might have to marry many times over before we discover the truth?' For the first time in our talk she smiled.

'Not at all,' I answered. 'We can stay with one partner through thick and thin. Lots of people do and for many reasons.'

'Do they find love, do you think?' Jennifer asked.

'I'm sure so, but some couples do actually stay together because they fear the unknown if they were to separate. Or they stay because of children growing up, or because of a guilt about leaving, or because they are oppressed and feel stuck in the relationship. Yet, I do believe some couples discover true love. However, we need the will to love and the love to will the marital journey. So, we need to choose our partner wisely. Unfortunately, when we are young that is a very hard thing to do. We are usually too young to know how to do it, although having said that it does seem that young people are marrying later in life than was the case a few years ago. That might reduce the risk of marital breakdown. "Falling" in love, as compared with loving, is usually followed by falling out of it. To love someone for their own wellbeing, Jennifer, and to put them first is true love in act. Many of us love with conditions attached. They may be unspoken or even unconscious conditions, but if they are breached our declared love can alter for the worse. I love you if you love me is not an uncommon silent deal.'

Jennifer left the office with no decision as to what to do for the best.

Perhaps at this stage of evolution the prospect of loving unconditionally in a personal intimate relationship or any other relationship for that matter is a far off ideal. Most of us have too many unfulfilled needs which prevent us from doing so. We expect and need something in return, even if we do not know what it is until we do not get it. The exception might be the love for one's child, but even that is open to question.

Admittedly, Jennifer and her husband were immature in their relationship, but their simple story makes the point. There are more sophisticated examples, but they boil down to the common question that if appetites are quenched or fade is there a true love waiting in the wings to fly to the rescue? What happens if there is not? Commonly, some couples do not even admit to themselves that their emotions have changed and they cover up the change with another holiday, a new house, or a child, or an affair.

Primal appetite still lurks behind the mask of civilised man. There is many a husband who believes he 'owns' his wife and that she is bound to him for life. The old concept of a wife as a chattel remains engrained in the male psyche. Mr Poutoir was not unique in his attitude towards marital rights. A man may bestow upon his wife all manner of affection and worldly goods, yet he does so upon his unspoken terms. His apparent loving generosity is conditional, so watch him bite if crossed!

On the other hand, there is many a hungry and manipulative wife who has made her bed and is willing to lie in it (and out of it!) provided she gets what she wants when she wants it. Private purposes live in most of us and we tend to keep them private, sometimes even from ourselves, until one day they rise to the surface hungry for fulfilment. The marriage we thought would deliver the goodies isn't enough. Appetite can be very self-possessed with its own private agenda intent on fulfilling its own desires and declaring undying love to its expected provider in the process.

APPETITE

Our personal appetites abound and, snakelike, they manipulate both ourselves and those we profess to love. We need to understand this process, not to reject our appetite, but to see it for what it is – a driving forceful energy bent on getting what it wants for as long as it wants it and making all sorts of promises along the way to get it – even marriage vows!

Do you truly love your intended one? Do you know what love is? Or do you merely 'love' the idea of getting married? Or is it that you cannot find a reason to say no? Are you drifting into marriage on the back of a long standing familiarity? Or is it no more than mutual physical attraction or not wanting to lose the relationship? Are you merely 'in love' – that euphoric emotional condition, which may be as long lasting as a risen soufflé hot out of the oven? Are you hoping marriage will mean companionship and save you from being alone? Will it make you financially secure? Are you in the last chance marital saloon?

Ask yourself as many questions as you are able to muster and try to be frank and honest with yourself and your spouse-to-be. Compare the difference between the level of relationship you already have in the bag and the extra responsibilities of marriage. Remember you always remain free to choose to tie the knot and probably you will tie the knot! But look through the glass of reason with the light on, not in the dark! At least you will walk down the aisle or visit the registrar knowing a little more about your particular recipe for marriage.

You might be thinking you could go too far analysing motives only to end up destroying the inherent goodness of your relationship. If that happens then you have saved both of you a lot of heartache and expense at some time in the future. If it doesn't happen you end up with no more to say and with the silent knowing that you are going to marry come what may. There will be some indefinable elusive knowingness of 'yes' that is more powerful than all else to the contrary. Your will to marry will have prevailed.

2

Gender

God created man – 'Male and female created he them.' But you do not have to believe in God to know that all of us possess both male and female qualities. The science of biology and genetics tells us that it is a proven fact. Observation alone demonstrates the myriad of male and female combinations. Obviously, a man is more male than female and a woman has more feminine attributes than male ones. Yet, only the proportions differ. Some guys are more 'feminine' or 'masculine' than others and likewise for ladies. The dominant masculine man and the submissive feminine woman were cornerstones of marital society for generations past, but are slowly becoming extinct as the passive feminine woman is being replaced by an ever increasing population of self-initiating and independent women. The balance of the sexes is changing and the rationally orientated man versus the emotionally orientated woman is giving way to a new order in personal relationships. Woman is now developing her masculine side and man is still reeling from the shock of it. In contrast to woman's increasing presence in man's world, he has been slow to tune into his inhibited feminine attributes. He is as the king on a chess board: slow moving, one square at a time compared with his queen's agility.

In philosophical terms male energy is seen as an outward bound force set to achieve a determined goal and make a point *in* life. Feminine energy is the receptive and sensitive aspect *of* life. These two 'poles' of sexual gender are essential to each other – the Chinese yin and yang, force and feeling, active and passive, the initiator and the receiver. However described, this interplay of male with female is co-present in everyone. Both are equally valid and depend on each other to achieve balanced human function.

Women have become active in walks of life previously the sole territory of men. An increasing number of men are becoming more accepting of their inherent femininity and man's 'macho' value is giving way to a more balanced type of manliness: one which embraces female qualities previously taboo in a man's world.

There is a need to be aware of this shift in gender balance. The proverbial 'battle of the sexes' flows from an inadequate interfunction between the male and female energies within us and between us. The mix of these male and female energies flow to and from husband and wife in the most concentrated of ways. This topic is not easy to grasp and observe in our daily lives, but it is of profound importance. Our primary marriage is 'internal', within each of us, male and female in one flesh. The more these two flesh mates function in balance, the more relational is the resultant individual. Of course, usually when we talk of marriage we are referring to the 'external' marriage between man and woman. However, it is in fact a secondary marriage, so to speak, and actually reflects for each spouse the degree of balance of male and female forces within themselves. A wife whose femininity is so pronounced that she prefers the role of being helpless and dependent upon her male provider, but who is also regularly dissatisfied with her lot, is yet to learn the need to develop her own male initiative. A husband who is particularly stressed with male driving energy and who habitually seeks to dominate his wife is yet to learn the need to be sensitive. Such a man has long since stifled his feminine sensitivities in the name of male egocentric behaviour. He has forsaken his sensitivity in order to drive forth into the external 'world' by using force without sufficient feeling – push without enough pull and action without adequate discretion.

It may take some time with much emotional water passing under the marital bridge before overt changes begin to emerge.

I recall a wealthy accountant client coming to see me. I had known him for years.

'My wife wishes to divorce me and take a degree in psychology,' he announced, waiting for me to be suitably shocked.

'Do you know why?'

'No. She says she hasn't loved me for years and that we have grown apart. She says I never listen to her and that she might as well be my mother with occasional sex thrown in and even that's no good any more. She says I make her feel claustrophobic. Personally, I think she is menopausal and has temporarily lost her senses. I have suggested she consults a psychiatrist, but she has refused. Is there a way to compel her to do so if she tries to divorce me?'

He was talking to me as if discussing a set of accounts requiring adjustment to balance properly. It is often the case that a client's attitude to their marital problems speaks volumes about why they have a problem in the first place. They bring it with them into the divorce court.

'Is that not the reason why?' I asked gently.

'What do mean?'

'Well, has your wife not given you her reasons? She appears to have told you.'

'Not at all. In my opinion her reasons are unjustified. They do not stand up to examination. There is no truth in them.' His reply was emphatic.

'Alan, if your wife believes her reasons are true then, provided your marriage has broken down irretrievably, she is entitled to a divorce.'

Alan grimaced a little. 'But I shall defend her allegations as ill-founded,' he retorted. 'Anyway, our marriage has not broken down irretrievably.'

'If your wife says it has then that is enough for the court. Defended divorces are very rare these days. Judges don't like them because if one spouse says the marriage is over that's it and deciding who might be to blame has no bearing on finances except in the most extreme of cases.'

'That's ridiculous!' Alan exclaimed. 'What about human rights?'

'You mean to be free of oppression?' I asked, tongue in cheek.

'I thought one had a right to a fair trial.'

'So, if you win your fair trial consider the implications. Would you expect your wife to be bound to you? To remain married and obliged to you come what may? Alan, she is free now to leave you if she wishes and start a new life and, in five years time, divorce you whether you like it or not. Gone are the days, Alan, when a wife was a chattel and beholden to her husband.'

'Suzie had nothing when we met. It's not right that she can now leave and take half my assets.'

'Is that what this is all about, Alan? *Assets*?' I asked.

'I don't follow,' he replied. 'I need a wife. This psychology stuff twists her mind. She reads all these books on freedom and how to be yourself and such like. Rubbish, if you ask me.'

He was ducking the money issue, but I didn't push it. Instead, I asked him, 'Have you discussed her feelings on these subjects with her? Have you shown an interest in why she is reading such books? Perhaps she is struggling to find a meaningful value for herself now the children have flown the nest,' I ventured to suggest.

'No, I have not. I told her in no uncertain terms that she's better off getting on with being a wife and not to become entrenched in emotional clap-trap.'

'Do you think that's wise if the clap-trap, as you call it, is close to her heart? You are saying that *she* is clap-trap if you rubbish her interests. A woman feels rejected and devalued when the man in her life dismisses her interests as worthless. They may be to you, but not to her. A woman feels life wholly. She doesn't naturally separate things out like we men tend to do.'

'Well, it's high time she did. All these self-awareness sessions of self-discovery are hardly wifely. In fact, I consider it to be an indulgence. If we hadn't attained a certain measure of wealth and security Suzie couldn't have these highbrow interests. They're pursued at my expense, in fact. Do you know, she says that I do not know her at all. Good Lord, can you credit that? Twenty-seven years of marriage and I don't know her? She was twenty when we married.'

'Do you *know* her, Alan?'

'Heaven help me!' he exclaimed with frustration. 'Of course I know her – every nook and cranny of her.'

'Well, you talk as if you don't know her at all. You might know how *you* wish her to be or how you have *believed* her to be, but if you *really* know her you would understand where she's coming from. You might even be interested in what she has to say. You seem reluctant to tune in to her needs as if they're a threat to you.'

'Look, I've spent my entire working life dealing in facts and figures. That's why we are where we are today. Suzie simply needs some practical advice to get a handle on reality and not this mumbo jumbo. Otherwise, she won't have the money to do it. She can get a job and support herself for a change. Damn it! She's only forty-seven. That would teach her.'

'After three kids now grown up and with your wealth, Alan, no court in the land will expect her to work,' I replied. 'Suzie will take a good chunk of your assets and maintenance unless you pay more to buy her out of it. Alan, you're the one who is living dreams. You can't make Suzie stay and you're a sitting duck financially. If I was you I'd go back home and read her books! You might learn something. You say you need a wife. Do you mean any wife or Suzie?'

'I need a wife who knows her place and appreciates it. I married Suzie thinking I'd got that but, oh no, she has to embark upon a self-searching trip leading to nothing short of desertion and betrayal. She's not the girl I married and I don't need or care for the so-called enlightened version. Getting in touch with your chakras doesn't pay the bills.'

Alan had always possessed about as much sensitivity as a tomcat on heat and he was running true to form. He did not relent and ended up alone and lonely with much reduced wealth. His kids see him occasionally, but he moans incessantly to them about how badly their mother has treated him. Self pity consumes him. He wines and dines a few ladies, but spends most of his time with them bemoaning his lot. Actually, he prefers it to coming into the twenty-first century.

The ego possessed male mind will perish unless it gets a handle on the feminine aspect of its own being. In my view, if Alan had been willing to show a real interest in Suzie and her need to re-evaluate herself they might still be married and be enjoying a more meaningful life.

The message for Alan is to understand the value of woman for herself as a person not just as a wife and mother. A fulfilling marital relationship requires a genuine interest in each other's *beingness* not just their *doingness*.

The traditional state of man tends to evaluate a person rationally by what they *do* whereas woman tends to evaluate a person 'in feeling' for who they *are*. The male talent is the *doingness*, but the feminine gift is her *beingness*. Without *being* there is no *doing*, yet Western society particularly has become preoccupied with the doing and our personal and internal beingness has suffered great neglect. No amount of material affluence and external success will solve the problem. It abides in the primary marriage of the male and female energies within each of us.

A client came to see me to make his will. I acted for him many years previously when his first wife divorced him. We discussed his will, which was complicated because he has children by both wives. Unless very wealthy, how best do you provide for your present wife without depriving the children from your first marriage of their so-called rightful inheritance?

After we had resolved the problem, he said, 'By the way, how would I stand if I divorced Janet?'

'You might fall over,' I replied.

'What do you mean?' he asked.

'Stanley, you have been married some years now. How old is Janet?'

'Sixty-one.'

'How much is your annual pension?'

'About £65k,' he replied, smiling.

'How much is Janet's pension?' I asked.

'She hasn't got one.'

'So, if there is a divorce,' I explained, 'Janet would no doubt apply for a pension split.'

'A what?' he asked.

'Janet would claim a share of your pension capital greatly reducing your income,' I said, 'unless you give her more of your free capital in lieu. But she might go for half your assets across the board, Stanley, so you could end up impoverished – at least by your standards.'

'Look,' Stanley said in a somewhat conciliatory tone, 'don't misunderstand me. Janet and I get on very well most of the time. It's just that every now and then she goes off on one.'

'Off on one?' I questioned.

'Yes. She gets in a big huff over nothing, but it can last for days, like when shopping for a tumble dryer the other day. I chose one and she blurted out in front of the saleswoman, "What's wrong with this one?" as she pointed to another make.

' "Nothing," I said. "I just think this is better".

' "Why?" she snapped back at me. "Why should it be better?"

' "No particular reason," I told her. "Have the one you like." I couldn't have cared less actually.

' "No, have the one you want. Don't worry about me," she said.

'I replied, "I'm not worried, Janet, but please do choose the one you prefer."

'"No!" she shouted and then walked off, leaving me feeling a complete idiot in front of the saleswoman. We didn't buy either of the wretched machines! Janet was off with me for a week.'

'How was the problem sorted?' I enquired.

'In the end, after a week of silent warfare, she must have realised I was on the brink of giving up. I was fed up with her antics.'

'What did you say?'

'I said, no matter how much I cared for her I was not willing to be on the receiving end of a life of habitual complaint. I told her if it carried on I would leave.'

'Wasn't that a little drastic?' I ventured.

'Not at all because it happens time and again and I'm sick of it.'

'Did she explain then?'

'She said it was because in the shop I looked at the various machines as though I was alone and her view didn't count. She felt superfluous and of no value. She said I do it a lot with her.'

'Is that true?' I asked.

'Yes, sort of in the sense that I chose one in my own head without involving her.'

'Did you accept her criticism?'

'I told her I hadn't realised she was interested in tumble dryers apart from using them.'

'That's probably true, but it's not enough to be right factually where a woman is concerned. Have you never heard the phrase – it's not enough to be right?' I asked.

'Janet said as much, telling me that her interest or lack

of it in tumble dryers is not the point. The point was that I showed no interest in her by going it alone as if she was not there.'

'That's a woman for you!' I declared.

'What do you mean?' Stanley asked.

'It's not what you do it's the way that you do it. Man's ego is self-serving; it rationalises its errors in self-defence. To relate to a woman you need more.'

'Pray, what is *more*?' Stanley asked.

'I mean a flow of awareness between man and woman. Man's ego ignores the flow and a woman knows when her feeling state is being ignored.'

'A woman can do the same. It's not one-sided,' Stanley said sharply.

'Not so!' I declared. 'The nature of woman's flow might change even to freezing point, but woman *lives in the flow*. Man struggles to find it.'

'Tommy rot,' said Stanley. 'You obviously don't know women like I do.'

'Sorry about that, Stanley. All I mean to say is if you had asked Janet which make she preferred then she might have had a view and told you or wanted to look at the options with you.'

'I'm not so sure,' said Stanley. 'This is all trivia. Let's finish off my will.'

'Stanley,' I replied before dropping the subject, 'I was once told life is made up of trivia, but is no trifle!'

Stanley nodded as if to digest such profundity, but he didn't so we completed his will.

I also recall a long suffering husband who almost withered to nothing in the face of his wife's emotional onslaughts. If, in her eyes, he fell short of her expectation of him she would remonstrate in the most reckless of ways; she cut all his suits up; she threw bricks at his car; she tossed his dinner across the kitchen or at him; on one occasion, she seized his testicles with both hands when he was naked in the bathroom and ran around the landing with him in tow. He had to use considerable force to break her grip, which intensified to produce excruciating pain whilst doing so. Then, with bruising to her wrists, she phoned the police. He felt embarrassed to tell the story and had no wish to have his testicles examined in his defence. He said they didn't show much external damage anyway.

The poor man asked me if he had grounds for divorce.

'Yes,' I answered.

'The trouble is,' he went on to say, 'I love my wife and don't want to lose her. Do you think you could write her a letter?'

'Along what lines?' I asked.

'Well, if you could say I had been to see you to enquire about a divorce because of the way she treats me, but I love her and really want her to change her ways.' As he uttered the words he looked weary and on the brink of tears.

'Have you thought of counselling?' I asked.

'She won't go near a doctor or a counsellor or any sort of professional.'

'What about a mutual friend?'

'No way,' he replied. 'I've spoken to her sister who knows how Linda is with me, but Linda just blames me for it all. I feel she needs to know I mean to sort things out one way or the other. She may take some notice if she gets a solicitor's letter.'

'Possibly, but it may make matters worse,' I countered.

'It can't be much worse and if Linda really thinks I'm going to end it she may just think again.'

'OK then,' I said. 'What do you want me to say?'

'What do you think?' Grahame asked. He obviously hadn't a clue what he wanted me to say. He naively thought a letter from me would do the trick. As if the mere sight of solicitor's letterhead is enough to rescue an ailing marriage. Usually it's the other way around; a lawyer's letter spells the end of the road whatever it says.

'Do you feel she will read it? Often such letters are binned unread.'

'I think she will read it,' he replied.

I switched on my recorder and started to dictate.

Dear Mrs Richardson,
Grahame has visited me very distressed regarding the state of his relationship with you. He has explained how dissatisfied you are with his behaviour and that you find him to be an unfit husband. He accepts that you feel that way, but believes the way you treat him prevents both of you from sorting out the problems. He earnestly wishes to regain your love and care for him. He tells me he loves you deeply and that he will do anything to make his marriage work. However, he realises that so much depends upon your will to do the same. Please, will you say whether or not you wish to save your marriage? If not, then albeit with a heavy and sad heart, he will take steps to end it. Please either write to me with your answer or tell Grahame personally.
Yours Sincerely

Grahame sat opposite me pondering my words. After a couple of minutes he announced in a very assertive manner, which I had not witnessed before, that the letter wasn't right.

'I know it was my suggestion, but on second thoughts the letter gives her the control again. She remains in charge, as if she can call the tune, as if the fate of our marriage is in her hands. I have always been on the receiving end of her – never the other way around. I think the letter needs to say that I've had enough and divorce proceedings are being issued. Maybe, if she sees I am willing to end it all, she will talk. If not, then at least I know where I stand.'

'Do you feel she knows what she wants?' I asked.

'What do you mean?'

'Well, many people know what they don't want – usually because they have it and they spend their lives protesting about it. It's easy to find fault and often people prefer it to changing things. There's a sort of perverted security in keeping it going.'

I thought I'd lost Grahame with such an explanation, but it's true. Many relationships thrive on nit-picking and fault-finding. I often think, if they were presented with perfection from their spouse, they would run a mile as the responsibility of having to relate to perfection would be a daunting task.

'Maybe, but that's her problem,' answered Grahame. 'If she believes the grass is greener elsewhere then let her go to find it. If you're right she might get fearful and have second thoughts.'

'Yes,' I said. 'But, Grahame, she might take you at your word and call your bluff.'

'I'm not bluffing. I mean it. I've had it up to here,' he said, putting his hand flat above his head.

'So then, how about changing the letter after "problems"

and saying...' I began to dictate again. 'Based upon the irretrievable breakdown of your marriage, coupled with your persistent and reckless unreasonable behaviour towards him, a petition will be served on you shortly and no doubt you will consult solicitors. There will be several matters to resolve, including a sale of your jointly owned house and a suitable division of your other matrimonial assets.

'How is that, Grahame?' I asked.

'Much better,' he replied.

The letter was duly despatched.

We need to become aware that male and female energies are co-present in each of us and function not only *between* us but *within us*, and this internal process changes balance as we develop and mature. For example, if a very passive angelic girl attracts a somewhat passive and inactive partner not much may get done once they are married, but it might be that one of them wakes up a little and becomes impatient of the lack of progress in the relationship. On the other hand, if that same girl marries an active and self-determined man he may become dominating towards her, taking for granted her compliance with him having his own way. As time goes by, she may begin to react emotionally to his domination and begin to protest. She may become less compliant and he might not like it. Another scenario may be that a 'bossy' lady marries a seemingly passive husband, tending always to have her own way. He may oppose her one day and disturb their apparent peace. Are they aware that the balance of sexual polarity is on the change? Often, these changes are interpreted as unwanted by one spouse or the other depending upon who is feeling the pinch! Actually, they are the very ground of progress if understood. Marriages don't stand still.

Grahame divorced his wife. She is now drinking heavily, living in Housing Association accommodation and driving other residents mad.

3

Love

Love is ever-present in the here and now of life, yet is often last on the agenda for everyday living. It does not impose upon us, and with infinite patience it awaits our realisation of it. It is a living power in each of us, yet we can fail to recognise its presence or to understand its nature and mistake it for some powerful emotion of intense liking, which does not stand the test of time.

Jennifer, whom I have told you about, came back to see me some two years later. She was still married to Colin, but had made up her mind to divorce him. She had undergone surgery and was very proud of the result.

'I decided that if the shape and size of my bosom was so important to Colin I would have it enlarged,' she explained with glee. 'So I got him to pay. Would you like to see them?' she asked, smiling but meaning it.

'Jennifer, thank you. I'm sure your bosom is fabulous, but I think it best you keep it under wraps, don't you?' I replied rather quickly.

'That's OK,' she said. 'I suppose I just want to show you my new found confidence. You know how upset I was last time we met.'

'I do indeed, Jennifer. Yet another man may have loved you just the way you were – bosom and all,' I said. 'To say the least, Colin was somewhat immature about love. Is he better now?' I asked, trying not to study Jennifer's now ample bosom whilst asking the question.

'Much better, but I'm not *better*, William. Colin doesn't love me now any more than before the op and I don't love him. The only difference is I know it, but he doesn't. I've told him I'm divorcing him and he's mortified. I've told him there are plenty of big breasted women about so go and find one. He's not having mine. Do you know, William, since the op I've realised that men go for shape, but women need a loving interest in them. And they make a fool of themselves trying to get it from the wrong guy. These days, the minute I suspect a man is over zealous about my body I go into reverse thrust.'

'That's an interesting way of putting it, Jennifer.'

'Well, it's true and my new man cares about me, but...!' she exclaimed, 'I'm going very slowly and I want a house of my own and no more marriage until I'm very sure of myself.'

'How often do you see him?' I asked.

'Whenever I can, but that's not often because he works away and Colin doesn't know about him. He's not going to know either. I want everything sorted without that complication. James is nothing to do with my breakup, but Colin would make a meal of it if he knew.'

Jennifer got her divorce and the house was sold. There was enough in half the equity for a deposit on a small terrace property and with a mortgage that didn't cripple her. Jennifer achieved her desired financial independence.

A little self-love goes a long way. Jennifer's life changed for the better once she acquired some self-esteem. It might have taken cosmetic surgery to kick start it but, once tasted, self-value is a must for self-confidence. When up and running, relationships with others, particularly lovers, take on a different flavour. The need to be loved will still be there, but not to the extent of being a doormat in a vain effort to get it, nor by kidding oneself that he or she is the one for you just because they are available.

Real love is committed to the wellbeing and growth of its beloved. It supports whatever is best for its beloved. Real love is not selfish; it does not seek to possess and control its beloved, but rather it nurtures and promotes their potential for improvement as a human being. It does it through each one of us if we let it be. But can we let it be? It might mean all sorts of sacrifices along the way and do we really love our so-called beloved enough to make those sacrifices? Is our beloved able to receive such love even if we are equipped to give it? Are we strong enough to sustain it without crumbling under the strain when our efforts are rejected? Do we first need to be loved by another in order to love? Are we hoping for it to be discovered mutually as we mature and cope with adversity? That is a wonderful ideal. Yet, rejection by one spouse may be fatal to a marriage when, understandably, the other spouse then turns away because the hurt is too much to bear. Then the inherent shortcomings of both spouses and their 'love' for each other are often revealed.

A husband came to see me not too long ago who explained that his wife had left him for another man. The husband was bringing home a net income well over £100k a year. He and his wife had a five-bedroom detached house in the Cheshire countryside. There were two children, the youngest being only eighteen months old. The other man earned about £30k a year and had left his wife and their two young children. He rented a two-bed flat and the 'lovers' set up home together. The husband was distraught with grief that his wife had deserted him and taken the children. However, he adjusted enough to the situation to establish a contact arrangement to see the children, but it broke his heart every time he collected them because he saw his wife looking lovely and he could not abide picturing her in another man's arms. He wanted her back at home.

After about a year he met someone else who cared a great deal for him. He responded to her affections and in the process broke the tie to his wife. One evening, when he was returning the children to their mother after a weekend with them, she asked to have a word with him. She announced that she had told her boyfriend to leave because she had realised she had made a grave mistake. She assumed her husband would be thrilled at this news and whisk her off back home. Alas, he told her that he had found a new love and that he was filing for a divorce because of her adultery. His wife was shocked and dismayed at the news. She felt her husband should welcome her home if only for the sake of their young children. She believed every effort should be made to restore the marriage.

I asked him if he had been maintaining the children during the separation.

'Yes,' he replied. 'Almost from day one I paid her £1,000 a month for the kids. I didn't pay for her. Why should I when she ran off with someone else?'

'That's OK,' I replied. '£1,000 a month for the children is generous. Did she complain?'

'No,' he said. 'Why should she as I was subsidising her living costs with her boyfriend? There's no way she was spending all that on the children.'

'I'm sure that was the case,' I said, 'but you're always

going to get an overlap at the higher end of child maintenance. It's often a problem, particularly when Dad usually buys all kinds of things when the children are with him for a few days: clothes, gadgets, toys and music – in fact, just about anything can be squeezed out of him if he's got the money!'

'Anyway,' he said, 'she's blown it now.'

'Yes,' I said. 'But didn't you feel you might have tried again with her if it wasn't for your new lady?'

'No. I realised I hadn't loved her for a long time. Our relationship took a turn for the worse after Katrina was born.'

'Is that your second child?'

'Yes.'

'Did you discuss your feelings or rather the lack of them with her at the time?'

'No, but I felt she knew we had drifted apart.'

'*We?*' I said questioningly.

'OK, then. *I* had drifted from her, but she did nothing about it. I felt she didn't want to do anything about it.'

'But surely it was for you to rescue things, wasn't it? You had drifted. You've already said you no longer loved her, whatever that might mean. You needed to get back on course. Otherwise, you were the one who should have left – not her. But you drifted and waited for her to do something and she did, albeit much later.'

'How do you mean?'

'Well, she left you.'

'Yes, but for another man. Not because of my drifting.'

'Are you sure?' I asked. 'She hardly went to a knight in shining armour. He was never going to match up to you as father of the children and provider. She was simply making a protest, although a foolish and risky one,' I said.

'There's no "simply" about it,' he retorted. 'She deserted me and took the children.'

'Was she supposed to leave them with you, then?' I asked. 'You are out working all day. You had already drifted away from family life. What was she to do? Desert the children too? No, she left you to your own devices, which is really what you wanted, wasn't it? A free agent to do as you pleased.'

'What are you trying to do?' He was becoming impatient with me. 'I've come here for a divorce, not to have a post-mortem on my marriage. My wife left me and she has committed adultery. That's all there is to it. Do I have grounds for a divorce?' he asked me, somewhat curtly.

'Yes, you do, provided your marriage has broken down irretrievably,' I replied.

'That's obvious. My wife has gone and I have someone else now. What are we supposed to do, have a threesome?'

'No, but your wife has declared that she wishes to return home. Therefore, she doesn't believe the marriage to be irretrievable. Only you do.'

'That's enough, isn't it?' he asked. 'It takes two to tango.'

'It's enough provided you are sure. You have two young children. You are both good parents and both of you have made mistakes. It is possible to learn from them to strengthen the marriage not to destroy it. Both of you are relatively young. It's a shame to deconstruct what could be a good and meaningful marriage and family household.'

He stared at me. 'Is this some protocol you have to adopt, to make certain I know what I am doing? Look,' he said, 'I have not made any mistake; my wife did by leaving me. That's the end of it. Yes, it might have been different if she had kicked the guy out earlier when I felt my world was crumbling around me and before I found someone new, but it's too late now.'

'Do you not think that by drifting away from her you started the landslide?' I asked in one final effort to get him to see the point.

'She didn't have to leave me,' he replied quickly. 'She could have stayed to thrash it out. She just kept on complaining about my lack of interest in her.'

'Why should she thrash out *your* problem?' I countered, but I knew he was not for changing his view of things. I carried on talking. 'All I'm saying is that it's not all her fault. You could have checked yourself when she complained to you. She would be a very unusual woman if she had not repeated her complaint a thousand times to you! Every relationship has its low points. Your new one will have its lows and you may be faced with the same problem a second time around. Life has a knack of returning you to the problem time and again until you tackle it properly and resolve it once and for all. It doesn't matter who the woman is; you will encounter the problem again when your new relationship reaches a certain stage.'

'What's the problem then?' he asked.

'Your belief that being so-called right is enough to justify yourself.'

'OK, so I prefer to solve the problem the second time around.'

That was that! He divorced his wife for adultery. She chose not to defend the divorce, but stated in an informal letter to the court that she did not believe the marriage had broken down irretrievably. She wrote that by her drastic mistake she had realised she really loved her husband.

On a general note, it seems to me that if we truly love we do so without any motive to gain. There are no conditions or restrictions. We respect the freedom of our beloved to choose their life direction and we honour their unique journey through life. We may offer guidance if we are fit to give it. We may offer ourselves to serve our love, yet we do not seek a return. We do not possess our beloved and we cherish and support their growth as a human being.

How then does this purist love of which I talk sit with marriage? Legally, if there is a civil ceremony, there is a contract. By the very structure of such a marriage, marital love becomes conditional, each party becoming obligated to the other to abide by certain terms. Religious ceremonies may also impose rules, again seeking to control and regulate the marital relationship, which may seemingly be at odds with the freedom of true love to function without fear or favour.

But marriage is wedlock! It is not by chance that we have such a word. Marriage ties us up in knots.

I shall move on.

In the following chapters some particular topics are addressed, which have cropped up frequently when tackling marital problems.

4

Children

Children crop up very frequently. Newborn babies are a delight to behold and, for many relationships, children serve to strengthen and affirm marriage. Family life is at its best when mother and father are at one, caring for and supporting their offspring. Particularly if the offspring grow to respond in kind with love and affection, good school results and develop a healthy set of personal values. Alas, this ideal family unit may be a far cry from actual family life in many instances.

The arrival of a child may change the flow of attention between husband and wife. When it was just the two of them their relational interest was, for the most part, towards each other. The addition of a little person in the fold can redirect a parent's emotional flow of personal attention away from their spouse to the child, and the 'deprived' spouse may feel the pinch when suddenly he or she is second in the pecking order. A childish reaction possibly, but the problem can be serious.

A young husband and father, who I shall name Andrew, consulted me to ask if he had grounds for divorce because of this very problem.

'It's become impossible,' he said to me, tears welling up in his eyes. 'Every time I go near her she says it's time for the baby's feed or she is too tired and I don't realise how much a new baby drains her of energy. When we go to bed she doesn't even want a cuddle. At weekends we're round at the grandparents and everything is, "Toby this and Toby that". I feel bad saying it, but Toby has taken over Sally's life.'

'How old is Toby?' I asked.

'Nine months,' he replied.

'Maybe Sally feels very fulfilled at present and needed in a unique way, as only mothers know when their first child arrives,' I ventured to suggest. 'Mothers do tend to be totally involved in their new offspring until the novelty wears off.'

'Novelty!' he exclaimed. 'I reckon it's going to be a long novelty.'

'What I mean to say is that a young mother is emotionally entwined with her child and it may take some time for her to find a balance between motherhood and being your wife, let alone being herself. At the moment it's natural for her to be finding her feet as a young mum. She assumes you are doing the same as a young dad.'

'But Sally is so into it. There is no room for me in a way. She breastfeeds for a start. I get to change him and hold him, but she has to check him every two minutes. She has to put him down in his basket, which Sally insists is in our room. It's ridiculous.'

'Don't you feel that the more you accept and share Sally's happiness at having Toby the closer she will be to you? The arrival of a child does change things, you know. A mother's love knows no bounds.'

'Yes and I don't count for much any more.'

'Motherhood is territorial,' I said.

'What do you mean?' he asked.

'Well, think about it for a moment. Toby has been growing in Sally's body for nine months. He is her flesh and blood. His body is of her body. Yes, man has the job of fertilisation, but it's a far cry from a woman's work of carrying and giving birth. If you accept that fact and involve yourself as fully as possible in caring for both of them she cannot fail but to love you for it.'

Give the man his due, he listened quietly and departed with more than enough to think about, but I felt he would be back. I had a hunch the problem was deeper than just the emotional upheaval of a new baby. Quite often I have heard an unhappy husband complain that, with hindsight, he realised his wife's emotions towards him changed after the birth of a child. And I have heard many a wife say her feelings for her husband waned following the birth of a child.

These symptoms speak volumes about the quality of the marital relationship. Deciding to have a child needs to be a real and well thought out decision by both husband and wife. Gone are the days when marriage equalled babies. Women are having children later than ever before. Careers, finances or just the pleasure of not being tied to the patter of tiny feet play their part in holding up the reproductive process. In an increasing number of cases women are choosing not to have children at all. The pattern of the traditional family is giving way to other marital values.

The arrival of a child is the arrival of new demands on the marital relationship. It is a joint venture between husband and wife and the investment is huge. Time, energy and money are required. Their lifestyle will change. Each parent needs to support the other in their respective roles as parent and, although the sharing of tasks is invaluable, if not only to break the monotony of routine, certain tasks are best suited to one parent or the other.

I recall one young mother saying she was convinced her husband was jealous of her breastfeeding the baby. I remember a young husband saying his wife was jealous at the fuss he made of his 'beautiful' baby daughter, always wanting to hold her and lull her to sleep. Nothing was too much trouble for him, yet the same could not be said for his attention to his wife.

Husband and wife need to understand how each other feel about starting a family. This question may seem simplistic, but ask it of yourself. Why do you wish to start a family? Is it because it is the most natural thing to do after getting married – the 'done' or 'expected' thing, so to speak? Is it to follow in the wake of your friends and not be left out of family social life as all of you move forward in age and circumstance? Or is it an earnest wish to bring into the world a child whose free will you will honour and whom you will encourage to develop their creative talents? Which motive sounds the most positive? To my mind the last demonstrates a wish to further creation in a real sense and not to have a child merely to satisfy a sort of emotional and habitual reproductive system.

Conceiving anything worthwhile requires commitment and dedication, whether it is a creative idea, a design, an invention, a new way of doing something or a new way of understanding. Why not apply the same, if not more, devotion to the decision to conceive a child? A husband and wife conceiving new life amidst their heartfelt lovemaking, with a conscious determination to reflect their love for each other, must surely be a more positive start for that new life compared to a haphazard, casual and reckless attitude to pregnancy.

In addition to this, it is now a recognised fact that an unborn child suffers the consequences of adverse parental behaviour during pregnancy; for example, because of drug or alcohol abuse. Such abuses are tangible enough to accept, but it is not as easy to acknowledge that the negative emotional condition of parents, either at conception or during the pregnancy, may adversely affect their unborn child. If would-be parents harbour ill will towards each other amidst their sexual encounters all manner of emotions can be generated between them. Contempt, frustration, anger, resentment, underlying rejection and even hatred may colour their emotional world as conception occurs. We see that our children inherit from us physical characteristics and often we observe traits of emotional behaviour in a child similar to that of one of its parents. The mix of male and female energies, which I have talked about earlier, accumulates through our ancestry and is handed down to the next generation in the reproductive process.

A child has the right to a unique place in the household. So, parents need to adjust and possibly change their ways significantly to accommodate the newly born addition. Marital life will change significantly. Family life, as opposed to married life, will take energy from the marriage into the wider arena of rearing offspring. Unless there is mutual agreement between husband and wife to start a family the value of the marriage itself may be lost. Energies move towards the children's needs. No more is the flow of energy and interest travelling exclusively between husband and wife, but rather from parent to child and child to parent. Whichever the direction, the power dynamic has shifted in favour of 'family' life. There are many who will say that this is what marriage is all about and the rewards are great joy and happiness. That may be so in many cases, but to a large extent only within the context of family experiences. There is a tendency for children, even when of age and independent, to take centre stage. The dynamics of the marital relationship give way to family life and the potential for the personal development of husband and wife is slowed down in favour of bringing up the children.

I have had several cases where a divorce has occurred late in marital life because the children have grown up and left home. The marital relationship had died somewhere along the way, masked by continuing family life activities.

Marriages which depend on family life for any significant meaning may continue into the grandchild era and as grandparents the husband and wife may have sufficient in common to sustain a lifestyle. Yet, such a lifestyle is not of the essence of marriage. A true marriage requires the primary devotion of husband and wife to the inherent spirit of its cause – a cause not rooted in the biology of life, but in the freewill to serve each other's development towards self-enlightenment. If that is to include having children, it is important to maintain marital supremacy – father and mother united with the children in their rightful place. Such a hierarchy is difficult to uphold when children's needs and their 'wants' have to be addressed. Particularly if mother and father are divided as to how best to do it. In the family arena the dynamics of male and female energies are diverse and those of the children tend to influence parental balance. In some cases one parent may be seriously at odds with the other when a child succeeds in dividing the camp.

I recall one distressed father leaving the household because his eldest son of twenty-four refused to leave home. Mother supported the son, saying it was his family home for life if he needed it. The son worked and could have afforded modest rented accommodation. However, he enjoyed his home comforts of meals, washing and the like, and mother 'loved' doing it. It was abundantly obvious that the 'marriage' had lost its way years earlier, if indeed it ever had a 'way'. The son had usurped his dad in the household; no doubt with Mother's unspoken support. Two years on they divorced by consent. The son took on his father's small outstanding mortgage liability and Father decided to leave his capital share in the family home until, as he declared somewhat tongue in cheek, 'death us do part'!

Most of us know of marriages where husband and wife have decided not to have children because they do not wish their way of life to change. They have no desire to worry about poor state schooling or the cost of private education or having to buy a bigger house. They do not wish to give up their careers or child-free holidays or other costly and time-consuming activities, which would be severely curtailed if a child arrived on the scene. An increasing number of people, for these reasons and many more, do not want to pay the price of being responsible for children. Also, some see around them the misery caused by parents who neglect their children – the conception of whom may have been amidst too much drink or dope and casual sexual indulgence. At least those people choosing not to have children are responsible enough to know that it is a major undertaking to have them and a commitment not to be undertaken lightly. There are more than enough random offspring in the world. Also, I often see people who can ill afford to raise their existing children, yet proceed to have more children regardless of the consequences.

Andrew visited me again to say things had got worse not better. Apparently, Sally showed him no affection at all. Her sole interest was Toby.

'I'm fed up, frankly,' he declared. 'Sally has switched off the light with me. Toby has it all. I feel redundant.'

'In what way?' I asked. 'As a husband or a father?'

'As a husband,' he replied quickly. 'Sally has no desire for me – no interest or concern. I reckon our marriage is over.'

'How are you with Toby?'

'How do you mean?'

'Are you involved with him? Does Sally welcome your interest or are you sidelined?'

'It's her and Toby, with me the visitor. It's not *us* and Toby. Sally has seen to that big time,' he said pursing his lips. He was hurt and upset, feeling family life was deserting him before it had really begun. A mother and young child have a bond forged in maternal biology and, if misused to exclude the father, it is a formidable weapon.

'I reckon she's determined to break us up. It doesn't make any sense though. Why have a child then destroy the marriage?' Andrew asked himself.

I offered a possible answer. 'Because sometimes a woman's emotional and sexual interest in her husband changes once a baby arrives. Maternal love consumes her and her sexual appetite dims amidst her new-found fulfilment as a mother. She no longer has an interest in her husband's needs. In fact, if he is needy of her attention and sexually demanding she may reject him. A mature attitude is required from the husband to bide his time and take the opportunity of becoming less dependent on his wife, but he may not be up to it. He could be childlike himself, needing all manner of attention, and his wife will sense it and may lose respect for him.'

'Are you saying that I'm like that?'
'Are you?'
'Maybe I was a little, at least over sex. You see, I'm more highly sexed than Sally. It's always been like that. It was always me who started us off. I never felt she wanted it like I did.'
'Wanted it?' I questioned. 'What about wanting her?' I asked.
'Well, you know what I mean, surely. A man needs the outlet and I get really agitated if I don't have it.'

Andrew departed from the office feeling he was returning home to a lost cause.

It has been said that blood is thicker than water, which implies, sometimes cynically, that family members tend to stick together defensively. Certainly, that can be so in divorce cases when parents of an unhappy couple take sides and make a difficult situation even worse. Close blood relationships are often beset with emotional bias, which hinders a resolution of the marital problem. Family life emanates from a biological process and its inherent influences are very strong. Marital life does not flow from a biological process – there is no close, family, biological connection between husband and wife. Indeed, it is illegal for it to be so. When children arrive on the marital scene the biased influences of biology arrive as well. This bias takes many forms as family life evolves. Many a daughter has idolised her doting and over-protective father to the extent that she is unable to cope with the shortcomings of her newly wedded husband. Many a son remains tied to his mother's apron strings, which retards his independence and ultimately tugs relentlessly at his own marriage. To add fuel to his marital pyre, he, in turn, is in the wilderness when his new wife fails to be as mother used to be in accepting his unsavoury domestic habits.

I have had several potential divorcees accompanied by Mummy or Daddy, explaining how they have done everything they can to help 'save' the marriage. Yes, everything instead of nothing, which really might have helped.

Before closing this chapter I should mention second and subsequent families. Inheriting children on remarriage can bring excessive weight into the household. This is not always the case, of course, as stepchildren are often joyous and rewarding additions to family life. On the other hand, they can be carriers of resentment, rejection and generally unacceptable behaviour. The so-called 'wronged' parent may use a child as an unwitting agent to cause as much havoc in the 'step-home' as they can muster. They feed the child with resentful and negative thoughts to play out in their new home environment.

The child's age is not particularly indicative of whether or not trouble is in store. A five-year-old can cause as much havoc as a teenager. I recall one difficult case.

Trevor had left his wife while she was pregnant with their second child. The first was five years old. Trevor came to see me when he received divorce papers. By that time he was living with his new-found love, Joan, who had three young children all under the age of six from a previous relationship. Joan had separated from her husband a year or so earlier and their divorce was pending. During contact visits, Trevor expected to bring his children, one being the new baby, into Joan's home to make an extended happy family. Trevor's estranged wife had other ideas. For starters, she primed the five-year-old with a multitude of complaints against his father. These complaints ranged from a lack of food on the table caused by Dad's financial neglect to his frequent 'abuse' of Mother, who had been left deserted to fend for herself. Dad had abandoned the family and the five-year-old who Mother declared to be man of the house to protect Mum at all cost – a tall order for a five-year-old boy!

This brainwashing did the trick nicely. When Trevor arrived to collect the children his young son opened the door, delivered an expletive to him worthy of the most seasoned barrack room banter and then proceeded to bang the door shut in his father's face. You might say Trevor received no more than his just desserts for leaving his pregnant wife, but from his perspective he had been living a nightmare with her. She had run up credit card debts, a bank overdraft, hire purchase and credit sales to the tune of nearly a £100k, steadfastly refusing to heed his pleas to stop. Also, she ceased taking her contraceptive pill without telling him then became pregnant and quit her job. And to put the tin lid on his side of the story, she attacked him violently whenever worse the wear for drink, which was most evenings.

'I had to leave her,' Trevor explained to me.

'Had you met Joan by then?' I asked.

'Yes, so I had somewhere to go,' he replied.

'Might it not have been wise to be on your own for a while till the dust settled? Another woman on the scene usually muddies the water.'

'How do you mean?'

'A woman scorned...' I said.

'Yes, but Joan had nothing to do with me leaving.'

'I'm sure,' I replied. 'But you won't convince your wife. It suits her to blame your infidelity for the marriage breakdown. She can feed the children emotionally with this blame. They see their mum alone, the fridge half-empty and treats reduced. They do not see the true reason why.'

From the look on his face I could see Trevor wanted contact with his children, not a lecture on how not to leave your wife.

'You have a chance with the baby provided you obtain regular contact, but you have your work cut out with your five-year-old,' I explained. 'I fear the damage is done. When a young child has been turned against an absent parent it is difficult for the court and welfare services to be effective. The hand that rocks the cradle rules the world,' I said pensively.

That conversation was about four years ago. Since then we have had fourteen court hearings and five welfare reports. For a long time the eldest boy refused to see his father. Trevor saw the baby for two hours a week. Birthday and Christmas cards to the older boy were returned unopened. Eventually, through Trevor's persistence, he saw both children at a contact centre once every two weeks and very recently it has been possible to introduce the younger child into his father's own home. Mother has tried to block contact whenever she has had the slightest excuse to do so and has only towed the line after being warned by the judge for contempt of court and the possible consequence of prison. Quite how that would have worked I didn't know, but perhaps the mention of it was enough to frighten her. Many a father would have given up the struggle long ago and it nearly cost him his new relationship. At one point he felt in the middle of a mother's sandwich. His partner wanted him committed to his new family life and to give up his quest to see his own children. His ex-wife, as she now is, wished to drive a wedge between him and his partner and turn the children against him. Trevor, in the middle, wished his children to be happy in the family household of his partner and her children.

CHILDREN

The story continues to unfold with his partner having just given birth to their first child. What a pecking order now!

There are numerous lessons to be learned from this not-uncommon tale of family dysfunction. Perhaps the most valuable relates to timing. Go gently in the way of new relationships when children are involved. Give time for acceptance and adjustment and do not fuel the emotional fires of an 'injured' parent by acting insensitively, however badly they may have behaved during the marriage. Remember children can too easily become pawns on the chessboard of marital unrest and their wellbeing amidst the crossfire truly needs to be protected as much as is possible.

5

Finances

I still have elderly couples visiting to make a will with the house and all finances in the husband's sole name and the dear wife knowing nothing of it.

'Oh, I leave all those sorts of things to Cyril, Mr Hood. He is far better than me when it comes to money.'

'But what about your pension, Mrs Brooks?' I ask. 'Do you not have your pension paid into your own bank?'

'I don't have a bank account. Do I have a pension, dearest?' Mrs Brooks asks, turning to her husband for an answer.

'Yes, Gertrude, and it's paid into my account for convenience.' Cyril looks at me. 'I draw enough for the house each week and pay the bills. Gertrude likes it that way.'

'Darling, it's never been any other way. You have always looked after me and that's all I have asked of money,' Gertrude announces with naive endearment.

Gertrude and Cyril survive from a bygone era, yet there are many like them – the classic picture of a husband in charge of finances unquestioned by his accepting wife, she having no wish to take responsibility for monetary matters. Gertrude wouldn't know how to operate a bank account, pay a bill or run the household budget. Cyril, however, had saved some £200k over forty years of married life. He had paid off the mortgage years ago and all Gertrude knew was that they had 'a few pennies put away for a rainy day'!

'We don't go out much you know, Cyril and I. We've always liked our own company and enjoy the grandchildren visiting. Cyril has always been good with money and we've been careful not to spend too much, haven't we, dear?'

Cyril smiled benignly in reply and, I thought, looked at me somewhat sheepishly. He wished to leave his dearly beloved wife a life interest in the savings as if they belonged to him.

'Gertrude won't know what to do with the money. It's best,' he explained, 'that she has the benefit of the interest and the children deal with it for her.'

However, after much open discussion, the house and the savings were put in joint names.

Isabella and her husband are a different story. Ten years into her marriage she discovered that her spendthrift husband had run up credit card debts to the tune of £70k. She agreed a second charge on the family home to pay off the debts and then he did it again. He bought designer clothes, high-tech gear, such as sound systems, media products and high-end camera and video equipment – nothing of lasting value.

'We've had one family holiday out of it, that's all,' Isabella cried. 'He has ruined our marriage. I've had enough. Am I responsible for his spending?' she asked.

'No, providing he is the card holder. The increased mortgage debt is joint, but that is spilt milk. Just don't agree to a second time around,' I answered.

'No way,' Isabella retorted. 'Actually, I don't know how much is left in the house.'

'Let's find out, then,' I replied.

We found out and the equity was much reduced. Nevertheless, Isabella had a struggle to persuade the court that she should not bear some part of the credit card debt.

'Surely, Mrs Brooks, you had the benefit of at least part of your husband's spending?' the district judge asked her at the final hearing of a protracted financial dispute. 'You are asking me to order your husband to take the entire burden of a significant liability, which will leave him very short of liquid capital. Do you think that to be fair and reasonable, Mrs Brooks? I'm not so sure,' declared the judge.

'Sir–' replied Mrs Brooks.

'That's all right, Mrs Brooks,' the judge intervened. 'I do not require an answer from you. I was merely pointing out my difficulty.'

'Yes, sir. But I do wish to answer your question if I may.'

'Very well, then.'

'The children and I had one family holiday out of all the money my husband spent. That is all. I never asked for the forty-inch television, the digital cameras, the all-round sound system, which cost in excess of £14k, or his other unending gadgets, which I wouldn't know how to use if I tried, but he did not heed my protests. He went on spending regardless, as if addicted to it. The first time he did it I agreed the extra loan on the house so I have that burden anyway. The second time was too much. I have a family to protect.'

'What do you say to that Mr Brooks?' asked the judge.

'That's rubbish. My wife knew we were spending and she had things as well. I bought her handbags, purses and the like. She never went short,' pleaded Mr Brooks.

In the end the case was decided on the need for a family home free of debt. So, in a way, Isabella won the day.

On another occasion, one distressed husband complained that his wife was abusing their joint account.

'Why do you have one, then?' I asked.

'When Anne and I first married we thought we should share bills and earmark our resources. Both of us worked, but my earnings were about twice hers. My salary was to go to the joint account and she would use her own to pay for food and household stuff. Everything else would come out of the joint account, regardless of who wrote the cheque or used the card. However, the 'everything' has changed a lot over the years. Clothes for us and the kids, the gym, school items, their music and swimming lessons, holidays, repairs to the house, car repairs, you name it – everything falls to the joint account. Anne's earnings are now well up compared with my income, which I admit has been a bit static over the last few years. Anne refuses to contribute any more, let alone pay her salary into the joint account. I dare not raise the subject now. She hits the roof if I do. God knows what she spends her money on, but it's not the family.'

'Why not redirect your salary into your own account and stop using the joint account?' I enquired.

'I threatened to do so not long ago and she said if I did I would live to regret it.'

'How?' I asked.

'I didn't ask.' He paused to reflect. 'I suppose I dread the idea of being on my own. I feel she might leave me. She seems more independent and carefree than me. I don't carry much weight any more.'

'Maybe you are more dependent on Anne than you have realised. How old are the kids now?'

'Sixteen and eighteen.'
'At school?'
'Just. Tom goes into an apprenticeship in September and James is taking his much-cherished gap year.'
'You've done your job,' I declared.
'What do mean?'
'Anne wants out now.'
'Oh really? And how can you be so sure?'
'I mean Anne wants out of the *habit* of your marriage. Either there is to be a fresh era or she will find a way to leave you. You have provided for her offspring. She has grown through her maternal years and is seeking a new purpose in life. Her reluctance to fund the joint account is but a symptom of her changing and independent values.'
'Maybe I'm redundant in her eyes.'
'Not quite so, but you could be unless you stand up for yourself.'
'How do you mean?'
'Well, stop your salary going to the joint account for one thing. Tell her that both of you have outgrown its use and that it needs closing. She can carry on buying the food and such like and you can pay the routine bills. All the rest you discuss. Both of you are then free to spend as you choose. Anne may not like it, but it separates you out a little. That's good for a marriage.'
'What if she refuses?'
'She is the one who is doing the refusing by not contributing to the joint account. All you are doing is sorting out the consequences. It is your call to redirect your salary. You don't need her consent. If she won't close the joint account then just let it be dormant or you can tell the bank and they will suspend it. It carries no overdraft does it?'

'Yes. It's in the red by about £3,000.'

'That's a shame,' I said. 'Joint accounts are a menace if they go overdrawn when a marriage hits trouble.'

'That's a bit strong. I wouldn't say my marriage is in trouble.'

'That may be so, but you have a problem to resolve otherwise you wouldn't be here. You would have decided with Anne directly how to handle the situation.'

Many a muddle over money serves to expose the true quality of a marital relationship. Only a mutual loving will to care for each other's wellbeing will sustain the relationship in times of prolonged financial hardship. When money becomes a problem the marriage is tested. If the problem exposes deceit or carelessness or reckless spending then, if not genuinely addressed, the facade called a marriage will fall apart. If a wife is with her indulgent husband primarily for the material benefits he is able and willing to provide then if they are no longer supplied, for whatever reason, she may head towards greener pastures.

In many marriages money appears to oil the wheels. When its flow stops the marriage grinds to a halt. Even in cases of enforced redundancy, long-term illness or a failing business, the resultant lack of money tests the marriage and the underlying character of husband and wife, which can be revealing. Emotions become frayed and affections may falter. The depreciating situation is made worse if there is no pulling together – no mutual determination to help each other through the difficulties. A negative spouse with self-pity can be more costly to a marriage than merely the loss of money or health or job. A loss of respect is far more serious.

I recall one case where the wife had become disillusioned because her husband had given up on himself.

FINANCES

'The problem is,' the wife explained with a mixture of tears and anger, 'Tom has declared his life is over and he might as well be dead.'

'Is it that bad?' I enquired.

'No, but Tom thinks it so. He chose redundancy at forty-five because of his heart and he feels worthless. He retires to bed at the slightest challenge. Even the gas bill upsets him.'

'It upsets me as well,' I retorted, trying to lighten things a little.

'Yes, but you don't slump into three-days' silence and bed, do you?'

'No, not quite,' I replied.

'Well, Tom does and it's as if I'm not there. He ignores me and no amount of cajoling helps. He reads the bible and that's it.'

'How do you manage financially?' I asked.

'Not very well. Benefits and some savings, which are in my mother's name actually. I know that's wrong, but they just serve to top up the budget, if you know what I mean.'

'Yes,' I said.

'Don't get me wrong,' the wife ventured, 'we have had good times. Tom is very well-qualified in chemistry and has travelled the world for his company, but found the stress too much in the end and his heart faltered. He had to take early retirement and his pension won't kick in for another three years yet. I can handle that, but not his defeatist attitude. It makes a mockery of our marriage. Lose respect and you lose love.'

Actually, I did not agree with her, but that made no difference. Francis left Tom and he died shortly afterwards. She picked up his pension death benefits and half his annual pension.

Be watchful of money's power of influence. Whether it is sparse or plentiful its consuming energy lurks in the shadows of marital life, sometimes to engulf its tender shoots of growth.

6

Sex

Man comes forth from woman and spends most of his life trying to get back in! A trite observation one might say, but how many of us actually analyse the elements of our sexual activity? Why should we when it can provide so much pleasure in abundance? Or does it? There are many tales of woe in the divorce world, let alone the misery which sex can cause generally when indulged irresponsibly. Unwanted babies, abuse, rape, addiction, promiscuity, pornography, prostitution, sexual slavery and its related slave trade, sexual bullying, oppression and a host of other unsavoury activities thrive across the sexual landscape of our so-called civilised world.

Whenever there is human appetite there is a trade to be had and sex is up there with the best of them. In this context, 'sex' means the many forms of physical sexual engagement which arise from the polarisation of our male and female elements, whether it be heterosexual, homosexual, lesbian, bisexual or a mixture of some other kind. Remember that every human being is both male and female and, whatever a person's sexual activity might involve, there is present within us and between us the interplay of these two primary energies.

The word 'sex' is probably derived from the Latin

'secare', meaning to cut or divide. The sexual reproduction process divides cells in order to multiply them. Sex itself is not a unifying process, but rather a polarising one enabling the individuation of life. This process is an *in-*division *within* the wholeness of life in order to create a multitude of different forms. As has been said in an earlier chapter there is one flesh, but many forms of it.

So, when one fleshly body meets another desirable body the laws of attraction are set in motion. *E-motion* then flows forth energising the appetite of attraction and becomes the strongest force of the evolving relationship. Here lies the trap. Good sex does not equal a good marriage. Emotions are unreliable when we believe they are necessarily long lasting. The flow of any particular emotional energy has a use by date. Thereafter it is on the wane and has to be transcended by a more sustaining power, otherwise the relationship will falter.

Very often, man's orientation towards sex is for its own sake and at odds with woman's deep need for a loving relationship. I am not talking about sexually active young women who seek, for the most part, the thrills and pleasures of carefree sex, but those amongst you ladies who really are searching for a truly loving and committed marital relationship. A husband is a house builder. His wife is a home maker. Even the word 'husband' derives from 'hus' (meaning house) and 'band' (meaning a ring or fence of protection). The wedding ring symbolises the man's promise to protect his wife and create their garden (a guarded place) in which his chosen bride may create their home. A man's preoccupation with sex hardly qualifies him for the role! He is lost to his true self, and his dependency on his wife's body for solace is no answer to his lack of wholeness. Likewise, the wife who uses her sexual charms to entice her husband into pliability for her own benefit hardly befits her true role as helpmate to man.

Flesh upon flesh seeks its own gratification. It desires to fulfil its own needs and is stimulated by the dynamics of sexual function. The participants usually become identified with the physical and emotional sensations associated with their sexual activity. Identification simply means that they become engrossed and 'lost' in the consuming sexual energy and forget other important aspects of themselves.

I had a case many years ago when I represented a wife divorcing her husband on the grounds of unreasonable behaviour. He had the habit of disappearing for days on end, leaving no word with his wife or children as to his whereabouts. His wife, Allison, was a most attractive woman in her early forties. The husband had a real problem of wishing to escape from domestic life and his escapades were very distressing to all involved. Sometimes he would vanish for weeks. Allison explained how impossible her husband was at home and that there was no meaningful family life.

'He leaves no word,' she explained. 'He doesn't telephone, the children are bewildered and I want no more of it.'

Allison divorced her husband and she remained in the family home. Financial issues were settled fairly easily, but what I didn't know until much later was that she continued to have a sexual relationship with her husband throughout the whole divorce process and afterwards.

'Why?' I asked Allison when she told me.

'Because it was only the sex that we both needed in our so-called marriage. Alan didn't want to be tied and I had no wish to live with an unreliable absconder. But we did hit the mark in bed. Sex was our common denominator.

It took us some time to face it. The rest of our marriage was a farce.'

'Including the children?' I asked.

'Of course not, but obviously they arrived through the sex. The problem for me after the divorce was stopping the habit. It's like an addiction. It was so familiar because we knew each other sexually so well, but eventually familiarity breeds contempt and I began to feel it as slavery. Alan would have carried on regardless, but how could I meet someone new when I'm in bed with my ex-husband every week?'

Allison did meet someone new and married him.

Her story is, in some ways, topped by another case I recall where the estranged wife was harassed by her redundant husband for frequent sex. She could take it or leave it. The husband was irregular with his financial support for the family, but as regular as clockwork with his demands for his wife's favours. She decided to charge him by the session – double his weekly maintenance payment, cash in hand – and he paid without quibble until she remarried four years later!

Sex stands alone as a powerful force to reckon with, but its emotional influences become entwined with other deep-rooted human needs, leading to confusion in many relationships. It is important to look at other values in a budding relationship; first, to see if they really exist and, second, to see if they are enough to warrant marriage. Being led by the sexual nose is no guide to marriage.

Yet unfilled sexual needs are, in themselves, emotionally charged with the desire to satiate them. If you find a willing partner with whom you are able to explore and give to each other the undoubted fruits of physical touch, warmth, intimacy and sexual expression there is much to be said for going for it. Just try to see the encounter for what it is and not necessarily a road to marriage. Remember appetite!

Marriages with not much more than sex to underpin them may come adrift when the symptoms of familiarity, boredom, disinterest, or even dislike slowly creep into the relationship. Husbands who tend to be on the outside of a personal relationship looking in are no match for their wives who *are* the relationship in feeling and by intent. Attention to detail is required by us poor men folk, otherwise we may lose the plot and possibly our wives.

Before ending this section it is important to cover sexual oppression and domination. Here, we return to the Poutoir case. Times have not changed that much even after forty years. Sexual abuse and bullying, often linked to domestic violence, as it is now called, abound in our society.

I remember representing an abused wife who visited me several times over a period of about five years. She would ask me piecemeal questions concerning divorce procedure and how much she might be awarded financially if she were to go ahead. She left the office on each occasion without deciding upon any particular course to pursue and I would not hear from her for months. Maybe a year would pass before I saw her again. In the meantime, I would think of her often, knowing she was unable to take the step needed to divorce her husband.

'You will never do it, you know?' she said, sitting opposite me.

'Do what?' I asked.

'Get me a divorce, of course,' she said, almost angrily.

'Why not?'

'Because he will deny it and make my life hell. I'll never be free of him.'

'Well, certainly, that will be so unless we try,' I said.
'He is so convincing. A judge would believe him.'
'It doesn't work like that,' I replied. 'The judge only has to believe you and then decide the marriage has broken down for good,' I said. 'That's all,' I added gently.

Eventually, she told me the whole story or at least as much of it as she could manage to describe. At the time, marital rape was new law, but if ever a case justified its existence it was this one. She was dragged, beaten and stripped of all self-esteem to the point where she actually believed her husband owned her and there was no escape. The first item on the agenda was to get him out of the house while the divorce was processed. He consulted lawyers who resisted, but under threat of a court order he left.

Then he sacked his lawyers and defended the divorce, denying he had ever laid a finger on her. On the morning of the hearing she failed to arrive at my office. I rang her home number.

'I'm not going through with it. Call it off. I'm sorry, but I can't do it.' She sounded resolute.

'It will work,' I said. 'Believe me – you will get your divorce.'

'Maybe, but then I will have to sell the house and I don't want that,' she said.

'No,' I replied, 'you will keep the house. Just wait and see.'

'No,' she said and put the phone down.

I drove the ten miles to her home and collected her. It was 9.15 a.m. and we were due in court at 10.30 a.m. I could just about make it. The fact that I turned up at her house made the difference and from then on it was relatively plain sailing. Her husband represented himself and made a complete fool of himself.

'Are you saying you have no knowledge, Mr Tomlinson, of your wife's scarring on her forehead?' asked the trial judge, pointedly.

'Yes, sir,' replied Mr Tomlinson.

'But your wife, Mr Tomlinson, says her scarring is due to you taking a beer bottle to her head.'

'That is a lie, sir.'

'Yet, Mr Tomlinson, you assert that you have slept lovingly by your wife in the marriage bed and her evidence that you routinely dragged her by the hair upstairs to bed to force yourself upon her is a figment of her imagination.'

'Yes, sir.'

'Then how can you have failed to notice her scarring if you have been lovingly by her side every night?' the judge asked.

There was a silence in the courtroom with all eyes upon Mr Tomlinson waiting for his answer.

'I don't know, sir.'

'You don't know!' exclaimed the judge.

'No, sir.'

Effectively, the case was over. When I rose to deliver my submission the judge merely said there was no need to trouble him. He took fifteen minutes and a coffee before delivering his decision. My client was awarded her divorce with costs and Mr Tomlinson was ordered not to return to the home.

The upsetting aspect of this case is the fact that the wife suffered for years on end before summoning the courage to change things. She was treated cruelly and reduced to a sexual object to be utilised upon the sexual whim of her bullying husband.

Sometime later she explained, 'I felt it was my fault every time he beat me. He would punch me and force me to do whatever took his fancy. It became so regular that I knew no other life and I built it into to my expected routine. The children never witnessed anything. In a sense they kept me going. I felt he was right. I realise now I believed that because he had a power that made me feel he was superior to me. I felt inadequate and lacking in authority to defend myself. I even believed he could kill me and get away with it. I would never be free of him. When we were teenagers I thought we loved each other and I gave him everything. Then, as time went by and we married, sex with me became his right on demand. He just expected it. I allowed it at first and then it became too difficult to refuse. His business failed and his aggression started as though it was my fault. I had surrendered to his power years before, so it was a line of least resistance for him to vent himself on me. I was like a rag doll in his clutches.'

The rot may set in early, and wives for generations past have been ashamed to denounce their abusive spouses. Women have been dependant on their bullying husbands for a home and they have been fearful for their offspring, lest they are deprived of financial support. They have believed it their duty to lie in the marital bed they have made and that their vows are indeed 'til death us do part' and 'for better or for worse'. However, these vows are not a licence for abuse and violence. Awaiting death as sweet relief lets both spouses off the hook of the responsibility of caring for themselves and each other.

7

Emotions

Emotional energy plays a vital part in our lives and relationships. The life force energy surging through us all is charged with all sorts of emotions. So what are they? I have to declare now to having had the benefit of learning a little about our feeling levels of life from a therapist with some forty years dedicated to helping those suffering from emotionally related problems. I mention this background because otherwise my readers might wonder how a divorce lawyer has gained such information relating to the subject.

All forms of life consist of energy. Whether the form is human, animal, vegetable, mineral, an idea or a thought, it is energy forming itself and behaving in a particular way. We now know as a fact of science that material forms are not in essence solid, but rather power energised to shape and form the material world and all within it and indeed our universe and beyond it.

This powerful energy has the inherent capacity to feel the state of itself, and as human beings consisting of such energy we also have the capacity to feel and also to be aware of ourselves. The conscious awareness levels of human beings vary tremendously, but most of us know the quality of feeling because we sense it, we are aware of it and we usually live by its messages. If something does not feel right we are uneasy. A mother feels for the safety of her child. The owner of a business feels the strength or otherwise of a deal brewing; however it looks on paper, if it doesn't feel right he or she is uneasy about closing it. A musician is sensitive in feeling to his or her cherished musical instrument and to the music played. A sportsperson is aware of the field of play and, depending on the level of awareness, is able to anticipate the flow of the game to gain the advantage. Feeling is the sensitive awareness of ourselves and each other and we would be lost without it. To state the obvious, our capacity to feel is a vital ingredient of our very being and is an inherent quality of every cell of our body.

Because we are feeling beings, we are sensitive to all that happens to us, whether good, bad or indifferent. We are as a pin cushion, absorbing the impact of our life experiences, and our feeling state is influenced by them and is moved in response. It emits a reply, so to speak – not a verbal or physical reply, but first and foremost a reply in feeling. That is an e-motional reply. The subsequent verbal or physical reply might be very different to the emotional one. Most of us know what it is like to hide our emotions!

When we encounter an experience we feel it. We have a feeling response to it and we are affected by it. We are no longer exactly the same in feeling as we were before the experience. It might only be a slight change with perhaps no significant consequence or it might be intense, as in suffering a major trauma or a joyous event. Either way, we become conditioned by the experience.

Getting married is an emotional experience. Loving exchanges are emotional. Arguments are emotional. In fact, everything we say and do involves emotional energy. We express ourselves emotionally and we react to each other emotionally. Yet, how reliable are emotional states of being? As a marital relationship is probably the most intimate personal relationship we are likely to encounter in our lives, it is of paramount importance to understand the significance of emotional energy and how it can conduct our lives often to our detriment.

The word 'emotion' itself implies an outward movement. All *e-motions* are feeling states, but not all feelings are emotional. Picture the waves upon the sea. Each wave is of the sea, but the sea is much more than its waves and below the surface is an ever increasing depth of calm. Winds may blow and disturb the surface of the sea, but not the calm deep beneath. So too is the case with human feeling and emotion. True feelings run deep while emotions are relatively superficial. Emotions are feeling states on the move. When the pond of our feeling world is disturbed in some way ripples of feeling move outwards and, as driftwood, we are often carried along with the flow. We tend to forget that we are more than merely our e-motional state and its powerful influence then reigns supreme. That is until the emotion subsides and other feelings surface in its place, which are closer to the truth of ourselves and which we would have preferred to follow rather than being swept along by the whirlwind of our relatively superficial emotions.

In a marital relationship some insight into the difference between feeling and emotion can be a saving grace. Emotions are notoriously unreliable when believed to be more than temporary feeling states. Once spent, a deeper reality may dawn. Essentially, an emotion is a reaction to an incoming stimulus. It may *feel* strong and true, and it is, but it is only true as to its own content. It does not represent the *deeper* you, and its strength lasts only for the time it is on the move and whilst its feeling content is coursing through you.

Many years ago I defended a wife charged with murdering her husband. At the trial there was a long debate about her state of mind. There was no evidence of diminished responsibility, but it was as clear as spring water that she was out of control emotionally at the time she plunged the knife into her husband's body. That did not excuse her behaviour, but it helps to understand the difference between the reactive behaviour of a person and the person. My lady client had been on the receiving end of very serious abuse from her husband for most of her long marriage and her violence gave vent to years of pent up emotion. Afterwards, she was distraught.

'I was filled with hate and disgust,' she told me. 'I was consumed with rage. I ran at him with the knife,' she said. 'I could take no more.'

She was mortified over what she had done. I could not imagine her harming anyone, yet there she was charged with murder. Emotions had consumed her and, after the event, she could not believe she had killed her husband.

'I should have just left him and stopped being a slave to him,' she mused. 'Now he has the upper hand. He's won from the grave. I am to be locked up again, but this time in a different sort of prison.'

I recall a distraught husband coming to see me who, via his business interests, I knew quite well. Clive had received a solicitor's letter saying his wife was going to divorce him for his adultery. He had met a very attractive woman at a business conference in Spain, but he was happily married with a loving wife and three young children.

He started talking to the woman when he was having an early evening swim in the hotel pool. She was on her own at the conference, as was Clive. They agreed to dine with each other and he explained to me what happened subsequently.

'I just suggested we ate together for company, out of the hotel, to give us a break from the business atmosphere. She agreed. I arranged to meet her in the foyer and when she appeared she looked stunning. I mean to die for! In the pool I had no real idea of how she looked and, frankly, I wasn't looking, but when she emerged from the lift she took my breath away. She was voluptuous, tall, slim and as sexy as could be. Anyway, we hit it off big time. We joked and talked of our families and our work. The evening raced on and walking back to the hotel we held hands. The grip became stronger as silently we enjoyed each other's company amidst the balmy Spanish air. She squeezed my hand and I did likewise until it felt as if we were making love through holding hands. When there was no room left for doubt about the message we were sending each other we turned and kissed. I tell you, the promises of the night ahead were all in that kiss. There it was on a plate and it felt so right to spend the night with her. When it was spent I felt differently. Her body became just a body. No more did I feel an intense desire for her, which I guess is the norm, until it builds up again. But far worse – I wished I hadn't done it. We both knew it was a one night stand, but, nevertheless, I felt I had betrayed my family's trust. I had undermined the integrity of my marriage. It would not be the same again. Something of its foundation had been eroded. Possibly, I was just feeling guilty and self-recriminating, but when I returned home I felt wretched and weakened, so much so that I consulted a psychologist to discuss the problem. He advised that I "share" with my wife, Anthea, the whole story and ask her to forgive me so we could start again unblemished, so to speak.' Clive looked as if he was going to burst. 'What a fool I was to follow his advice!' he exclaimed. 'Anthea couldn't take it. My confession hurt her too much. She would not touch me or come near me. Even the kids seemed estranged from me. I was lost and I felt powerless to retrieve the situation. Anything I said made it worse. Anthea demanded I move out and so I did. I felt I had no standing to remain in the house and here I am faced with divorce. I've lost my family because of one night's folly.'

Both these tales of woe show how emotions, albeit valid and apparently 'real' in their moments of influence, can lead to disaster. On a minor scale, mini disasters happen every day when we say or do things we regret, especially if to our beloved. A quick tongue, a violent move or a silent mood can all disturb the balance of the precarious world of married life. Yet, beneath our emotional life is a more reliable and stable reference manual. In basic terms, it might be described as a gut feeling of how to behave for the best amidst life's game of snakes and ladders. In refined terms, one might say it is an intuitive feeling of truth, which offers guidance to us along the narrow way to happiness and consistency.

This intuition is beneath the waves of our emotional highs and lows, of temporary distractions and of knee jerk reactions to outside encounters. A useful beginners' guide is to recognise that our emotional response or, more accurately, our reaction to a situation, whether it be an event or a person's behaviour or, for that matter, any kind of stimulus to which we are exposed, is going to be one of three types – pleasurable, painful or one of indifference (although indifference does have a bias, however slight, towards either pain or pleasure if reflected upon carefully).

Human nature tends to move towards a pleasurable stimulus, but away from a painful one. However, on many occasions, the opposite response is needed. Sometimes we need to resist a pleasurable opportunity. Such an opportunity does not necessarily lead to joy and happiness. Conversely, we may need to affirm an emotionally painful encounter and face it and deal with it, otherwise it might return to haunt us later in life, albeit in another guise as unfinished business. We need to face our demons and these demons may be deep rooted.

Human beings have become conditioned by their life experiences and of those before them. Through the ages, the long body of mankind has been moulded by its evolving processes and we are full of defensive reactions to life's encounters. This conditioning severely restricts our freedom to choose our response. Instead of embracing life around us, we can find ourselves rejecting it if it does not suit our biased expectations.

Returning to my two case histories, my enraged lady client was acquitted of murder, but the jury found her guilty of manslaughter. She served eighteen months in an open prison. Clive was reunited with his wife, but not before she put him through the spiked hoops of a woman scorned. She withdrew her divorce petition at the last minute having told him she was definitely going through with it. In Clive's case appetite and emotion had combined to lead him into a temptation, which almost proved to be the undoing of his marriage and family life.

Before leaving this chapter, it is worth a word or two about how to deal with emotional energy when it is inhibited and builds up within us excessively. Emotions are fine when handled intelligently, but often we hold back for whatever reason from dealing with them adequately and they gather momentum. This is particularly so when we feel we have been wronged and unjustly treated or when we are harbouring negative feelings about our partner that we are fearful to express in the open. It is helpful to talk them through with someone in whom you are able to confide. Women are infinitely better at this practice than men because men, as rationally orientated beings, tend to want to work things out in their head. Women, as feeling beings, are able to tap into their emotional complexes more readily. However, whether it is man or woman, suppressing negative emotions out of sight and mind can lead to quite serious depression. Admitting and verbalising one's emotions, with no holds barred in a safe place with a faithful friend, can help considerably. Ideally, one's spouse is the best confidante, but if the subject matter is very sensitive and relates to your marriage or marriage partner then to open up to your spouse requires a high level of understanding and acceptance of each other's emotional complexes. Both of you have to understand that whatever is expressed verbally it is an emotional condition only and does not represent a threat to the relationship. Otherwise, one may provoke personal offence, which in itself becomes the subject of an emotional reaction by the other spouse. The spiral of reactivity between partners can then escalate out of control.

There are many cases of emotions being suppressed to the point of actually causing depression and other illness. Negative emotions (resentment, dislike, regret or anger) may feel too difficult to face, so we try to push them out of sight, but their energy remains in our system. It may take counselling or therapy to resolve the problem.

8

Opposition

By the time a client arrives in my office for advice regarding divorce the writing is on the invisible wall, which is already the hardened barrier against any prospect of reconciliation. In most cases, therefore, any talk of reconciliation is short lived because, usually when I first meet the client, the 'marriage' (as the law would have it) has broken down irretrievably. Marriage guidance, if sought, has already proved to be next to useless and the trenches of defence of both parties have been dug to warlike standards.

Therefore, consider for a moment a client's reaction to my suggestion that, as far as William Blake was concerned, 'Opposition is true friendship', and that it might be worthwhile reviewing one of the purposes of marriage before ending it.

'What on earth are you talking about?' asked Jack, bemused at my excursion into amateur philosophy. 'Do you seriously believe that I should stay with my lunatic wife because it's good for me?' Jack considered himself to be of the philosophical type and highly intelligent with mere mortals far beneath him, hence my reference to the late Mr Blake. I thought it might appeal.

'Let me get this straight now,' said Jack after I had further explained myself. 'You are advocating that one's spouse should give you years of grief to aid one's development and that a wife's constant nagging should be seen as assisting her husband in breaking through his ego structure, thereby setting him free from its tyranny over his true self? Also, that man's resistance to his wife's excessive demands and wants serves to aid her gaining self control? And to boot that, a husband's egocentric behaviour towards his wife wakes her from the sleep of feminine passivity enabling her to challenge him? Have I got that right?' Jack was visibly excited at having found new mind-fodder, no doubt to debate endlessly.

At this stage, I need to tell you that I had known Jack for years when he came to see me and I knew that he could bore the rational pants off the best of *Mastermind* let alone his wife's – had she worn any. Jack is a longstanding member of Mensa, which I suspect is the last qualification for married life when it comes to relating to the dancing mind of woman.

'Was it not the wife of Socrates – the most nagging wife in all Greece – who enabled him to defeat every opponent in debate?' I retorted with conviction. 'The most rational of men are no match for the speed of a woman's intuitive insight. She sees the limitations of his ego even though she might not say so for fear of reprisal.'

'William.' Jack uttered my name as if about to scold me. 'You have spent most of your legal life divorcing folk, presumably advocating they have no moral, ethical or religious obligation to remain married when their problems are seemingly beyond marital redemption, but now you promote masochistic marital disharmony as a way of life,' Jack pronounced calmly.

'I have read, Jack, that Mr Blake's words might be modified to say that *intelligent* opposition is true friendship,'

OPPOSITION

I retorted. 'All I am suggesting, Jack, is that one might retreat from a marriage too early and not learn the lessons that it has to offer. A very wise man once wrote that marriage teaches us who we are not. The true self being slowly eked out of our personal closet as our efforts at maintaining a pseudo image crumble in the face of marital adversity. If we accept that life is a developing process then our relationships – particularly our personal relationships – are central to that process. I believe that the errors or lack of insight, which lead us into marriage, need to be thoroughly realised and understood before we end it otherwise we tend to repeat the error. Actually, I have acted for clients when their second or third marriages have come unstuck for very much the same reasons each time around. The theory that 'opposites attract' is not without foundation. On the one hand, the attraction of a challenging and stimulating relationship brings the two people together and, on the other, it reveals their differences, which they can learn to reconcile and accept as marital time passes. The dynamics of such a relationship can be very rewarding if they stay the course.

When two people of similar temperaments get together, the stimulus value can be low. They like the harmony found in similarity, but the dynamic of opposition can be lacking and their development potential becomes limited unless one of them pushes out the boundaries. Either way, without opposition the relationship may become stagnant. I rest my case,' said I with a smile.

Jack sat there for a moment silently. Then he started. 'So you believe that friction between husband and wife can be a good thing? Is that right?'

'Yes. If used intelligently it aids self-examination. I do not mean that one should suffer blindly until death;

although, of course, people do just that. I mean that healthy opposition to one's views or habits or behaviour can be a good thing. Instead of merely rejecting the apparent conflict, it can be used to examine one's behaviour to see if there is room for improvement. Usually there is room.'

'You mean the nagging, complaining and demanding wife may have a point?'

'Yes, if only to expose your vulnerability to a feminine challenge and your resultant lack of self-control. You say yourself that you cannot abide Janet's constant fault-finding, but how do you deal with it, Jack? Do you close down, go out to the pub, try to placate her or face the music head on and practice self-control?'

'Face the music!' Jack exclaimed. 'I have her records of complaint emblazoned upon my soul, thank you. Her nagging voice echoes in my ear. There is no satisfying her.'

'Jack, men make the error of believing they should be able to satisfy a woman. What they do not realise is that the power of femininity is infinite. It does not wish to be satisfied. It wants what it wants when it wants it. Man has to learn how to handle the shopping list. Nagging was born out of woman's frustration with man's preference for serving anything but the needs of woman. Therefore, he often caves in to her wants to keep her quiet for a while. He does not have enough interest in her needs to truly relate to her properly. He prefers easier tasks, such as sport, business, drinking, television, gardening, the children, cars, boats, affairs or whatever.'

Jack retorted instantly, 'The more you relate properly to a woman the more she wants from you. She likes the attention and then comes to expect it so when she doesn't get it the nagging is worse. I've tried all that devotion stuff.'

'Jack,' I said, '*needs*, not *wants*, and anyway attention is not enough.'

'Really?' Jack muttered.

'Yes, really,' I said. 'Active interest is the key, Jack, with mind, soul and body *then* you have the beginnings of devotion.'

'The beginnings!' Jack exclaimed. 'Where's the end?'

'There is no end. It is an evolving process and we see how far we can get,' I replied. 'Woman is the gateway to the new wine of life. She is the fountain and the means of finding its source. An interest in woman is an interest in the substance of life. To be interested you have to be *in*, but to show attention you merely have to be *at*.'

'For God's sake! That's too deep for me.' Jack was nodding his head saying a big 'no' to my rare description of woman's hidden secrets.

'OK,' I said, realising that I was moving into uncharted waters. 'Suffice it to say, Jack, if you devote yourself to your wife with absolute interest in her she will either respond with love and great joy or depart in fright. You cannot lose. If she stays, you have a treasure chest of feminine riches and if she leaves, you are spared the stony ground.'

'I think I've got stony ground,' Jack said solemnly. 'Sometimes, you know, I've nearly bashed her. She's so unreasonable. Where does that put me on the scales of interest?'

'Man's violence to woman is rooted in deep-seated anger, frustration and defence,' I declared. 'When the cork of restraint pops the bottle there are many men capable of the most heinous of offences against the fairer sex.'

Jack retorted, 'I only meant I have felt like slapping her face.'

As we know from science, it is opposing forces that make the world go around. Without gravity we would have no earthly stability. Without a balance of forces through opposing tensions there would be no creation. Life is dynamic and that includes human relationship. Opposing ideas, feelings, thoughts and actions are inherent in everyday life for us all. Yet, often in our personal relationships we seek the comfort of acceptance from our partner to be without question or objection. We believe there is enough wrangling to cope with in the big wide world and home should be a relief from such strife. Yet, in many instances, home is a breeding ground for argument and disharmony.

However, it is not opposition that is the culprit. It is our reactive nature to each other's opposition that escalates friction in the household. If we learn to say 'yes' to our partners' contrary views and ways and accept their validity from their perspective before we embark on challenging them we avoid the rejection syndrome. So often an expressed view or opinion is dashed to the ground by a reactive counter such as, 'Don't be stupid,' or 'You don't know what you are talking about,' or 'For God's sake, grow up.' Worse still is the opinionated spouse who declares, 'No, I forbid it, and that's the end of that!' leaving the timid recipient with no space left to move, let alone retreat.

This dismissive behaviour in a relationship feels like a rejection of our worth and value – indeed, a rejection of our self as a person. The baby is thrown out with the bathwater. Healthy differences are to be affirmed as progressive and enriching of the relationship, inviting debate and examination. Self-entrenched opinions demanding subservience have no place in marriage. And by 'opposition' I do not mean the forceful imposition of one spouse upon the other, whether physical, emotional or ideological.

Passionate disagreements and debates may all be countenanced within the mutual love and acceptance of each other as worthy and valuable marriage partners.

9

Age Difference

There is something inherently exciting about personal and intimate relationships with significant age differences. An older fellow may find a younger woman sexually stimulating and a trophy to display upon his ageing arm, and she may feel secure and able to rely on his maturity and established lifestyle. A young man may find an older woman tantalising and irresistible. An older woman may find she enjoys the freshness and inexperience of a younger partner. She may relish having the upper hand, while he savours the fruits of her more experienced ways. These somewhat superficial observations do not, of course, embrace the possibility that true love brought the couple together or has developed as the relationship grows.

    A good friend of mine once dated a woman some twenty-five years older than him. He was convinced he loved her. The lady concerned was glamorous and beautiful and in her early fifties. Divorced from a very wealthy gentleman, she had her own home and a generous settlement. My besotted friend felt their relationship to be timeless, and moved in with her amidst ecstatic happiness. She gave all to him – overflowing with passions kept under wrap during her marriage. She had told my friend that she had been unable to express herself in the stifling relationship endured with her dominant husband. Now, with her newfound lover, she felt safe and able to give herself, mind and body, into his caring arms.

And so his life unfolded in this idyllic setting of loving happiness. His professional life as an accountant prospered amidst luxury holidays, classy cars and other material pleasures, mostly funded by his amorous and generous lady. Today, however, we are thirty years on and she is an ageing eighty-three-year-old. My friend is a young sixty-five! They did not marry, which is telling in itself. Recently he confessed that the strain of the age difference was finally telling on him.

One might say very readily that he made his comfortable bed thirty years ago and should continue to lie in it. However, he feels the next ten years are his best to come because he is retiring and can expand his horizons, but, alas, not with his beloved, but old, lady. She has become demanding and forgetful and wishes to leave the bulk of her assets to her grandchildren by her marriage. She feels that her much younger partner is well-heeled on his own account except that, after her death, she will allow him to remain in their home until he dies or remarries. He wishes to leave her while she remains able to take care of herself and then her daughter will have time to step in slowly and take the reins if her mother becomes infirm.

This short summary may be contrasted with a similar story, but this time the roles are reversed. The lady is a vivacious sixty-three-year-old with energy in abundance and her husband is eighty-five. She finds her husband's old age frustrating and limiting, but she loves him dearly. Her love has transformed itself over the years, adapting to the changing dynamics of the relationship. Essentially, if one strips away all the frills the change is from lover to carer. Yet, there is as much love in the caring as there was in the passion of earlier years.

Younger readers may be aghast that I describe a sixty-three-year-old as vivacious and full of energy, but it is true nowadays for so many people. No wonder the State has raised the pensionable age!

I have hardly carried out a statistical survey, but these two examples, together with others I have witnessed, are informative. It seems the case that a woman's capacity to love a man through the changing years and dynamics of a personal relationship leaves most men standing in the shadows when it comes to reciprocating. Women have a unique capacity for caring for their elderly and infirm husbands.

Nevertheless, there are many ageing marriages where the couple grow old gracefully adoring each other. Beauty is in the eye of the beholder.

My grandfather, at ninety-four, told me regularly that his darling Edith, who was ninety-two, was as beautiful as the day he married her. Such beauty is fathoms beneath skin deep. Similar ages provide at least a more level playing field for husband and wife to stand the tests of ravaging time.

Underlying all debate concerning age differences in personal relationships abides the truth that real love takes no heed of age or physical condition. True love is consistent through changing times and conditions, including human ones, yet it remains timeless and unconditional. So, if you embark upon a relationship with someone much older or younger than yourself, be prepared for time to catch up with you and then handle your relationship with care. Do not confuse your waning appetite for your ageing partner with your underlying love for them. Love in act adapts to changing times, but love itself never dies.

An aspect of relationships, concerning age, which does not arise from a significant age difference, is the husband who leaves his post-menopausal wife for a younger model. There is still an ageing problem, but of an ageing imbalance rather than of an age difference. Men seem to fare better in the ageing stakes compared with the ladies. Many men improve with age, whereas women may lose their shape and with it their feminine ways.

One male client and close friend, who I have known well for more than forty years, explained, 'Look, I love and care for Elizabeth and she will want for nothing financially, but I just do not wish to be with her any more. We are a spent force. Elizabeth has lost interest in herself as a vibrant woman. She is a wonderful mother and spends most of her time indulging the kids and pampering to their needs. As a wife she has lost the plot. There's no excitement; no putting "us" first and, worst of all, there is no chemistry between us.'

'Well,' I said, 'if love is dependent upon chemistry it cannot be true love. True love is not dependent on anything. Love is. You either have it or you don't.'

'Really?'

'Yes – really. All you are doing now is searching for a replay of times past with a younger model to stimulate you because you are ageing. Viagra's a cheaper option.'

'That's ridiculous. It's not a sex stimulus I need, but a life stimulus. I want Sarah because she makes me feel alive. She is interested in me. She energises me.'

'Exactly,' I said.

'What do mean?' he asked.

'Elizabeth energised you once upon a time. Perhaps now she needs a spark or two from you, but that would mean you finding the key for a change of orientation towards her. I suspect Elizabeth needs a stimulus as much as you do.'

'OK, maybe, but I have not got the key and there's no point in us being miserable together,' he answered defensively.

'Perhaps if you are both miserable together the two of you might find new values in your relationship, which will be equally if not more rewarding than those past. I venture to suggest that with your intended new model that is unlikely to be the case.'

'You are an idealist,' he replied. 'I'm not staying with someone–'

'Someone!' I exclaimed. 'This "someone" is your wife. You have three children by her. You have been together for thirty-odd years and now she is reduced to "someone". Is that all that's left?'

He paused, but not for long. 'Actually, that's right. The history is there – a good history at that – but that is all. Now I need something new, which I've never had with Elizabeth and I want it before I'm too old to appreciate it.'

'What's that?' I asked.

'It is the chance to give without obligation or the need to provide for family life. And for my giving to be received joyfully and with no expectancy. It is a simple delight to be able to do it freely and to be loved for it. I have the wealth now and can be around all day to enjoy it with Sarah. When Elizabeth and I were young I was struggling to make it. In fact, it is only since we sold out that things have changed. The pattern was set with work for me, and the kids for Elizabeth and her girly lunches and what have you, which she still thrives on.

'Sarah has next to nothing except for her beauty and

everything we do is new to her. I love buying her clothes and seeing her dress for dining out and we love travelling. But there is no demand from her; the process of giving and receiving simply flows between us. Look, I have no illusions that if I could not give her the lifestyle we have together she would not be with me, but her happiness is genuine and I feel that, in many ways, she really loves me. If I was as ugly as sin and decrepit she would not be with me whatever my money could buy her. Anyway, doesn't a woman tend to love a man who cherishes her and provides for her? We plan to buy a small place maybe in the South of France and spend time there.'

I have heard since that my friend spent far more than he intended on his 'small place' in the sun. Apparently, Sarah chose a splendid villa with ocean views and enjoys inviting her young English friends for staying visits on a regular basis.

10

Religion

Is religion a hazard in marriage or a godsend? Many people would say it can only serve to enrich a relationship. However, the subjective interpretation of religious beliefs may cause marital conflict, particularly if there is a mixed marriage of faiths or denomination, and certain aspects of one spouse's religious culture may not be acceptable to the other spouse.

All major religions include at least some form of marital code and certain religions have a stricter approach to marriage than others, with long-standing established rules to regulate conduct, both during the marriage and in the event of divorce.

The laws of Islam, based upon the Qur'an and the civil laws of certain Islamic-based countries, combine to govern the tenure of marriage and the rights and obligations of husband and wife. The State of Israel has no civil marital law, but adopts the laws of Judaism. In Israel, only a properly constituted religious ceremony is valid. There is no civil procedure applicable in Israel; whereas, in most Western countries, a religious ceremony alone does not make a marriage valid and binding in law. A civil process is also required.

There is the traditional practice of arranged marriages

in both Islamic and Hindu religions. 'Love' marriages are on the increase, but the traditional school still believe arranged marriages produce greater stability. Arranged marriages are usually of a couple from similar backgrounds and take place only with their consent, with the 'matching' process being very thorough.

The Buddhist marriage is different again. There is no religious connotation, but rather a social union whereby each spouse is advised to follow certain social guidelines, which uphold the respect and caring for each other's wellbeing.

The Christian religion has many sectarian denominations, some more regulated than others. For example, it might be said that the Protestant view of marriage is more liberal than the Roman Catholic stance on marriage, particularly when one compares the Vatican code with, say, the Church of England.

Nevertheless, whatever one's religious beliefs may or may not be, the fundamental qualities of humanity are the same. We are all of male and female composition. All of us possess an appetite for something or someone and, whether or not it suits our private purposes in life to accept it, love is an ever-present power amongst us. Alas, private purpose in humanity abounds and we only have to watch, hear or read the news media to see how subjective religious doctrines are vented in a myriad of ways and how political and social ideals may squash the goodwill of man towards his neighbour. Many of these ideals are born of religious belief, but the preferred form of these beliefs can drown the true meaning of their origin.

I recall one lady being very distressed that her husband did not believe in God.

'Surely,' I said, 'you must have known this when you married him.'

'Yes. I felt he would change given time, but he says I try to cajole him into coming to church with me when it means nothing to him.'

'Then, why not let him be?' I asked tentatively.

'Because I feel uncomfortable with a man who rejects God and he's a heathen!' she exclaimed.

'Surely, you have to believe in God before you can reject Him,' I replied. 'Anyway, perhaps he just does not believe in the God you talk of, but maybe he has his own idea of God. Possibly you are not leaving him free to find God. Do you mind telling me your faith?' I asked.

'Roman Catholic,' she replied.

'Do you think if you suggested attending a non-catholic church, such as Methodist, it might help?'

'Are you a Methodist?' she enquired.

'No,' I answered. She looked at me for a while expecting more. She couldn't resist one more question.

'Which church do you go to, then?'

'Any that will receive me,' I answered.

'Any?' she quizzed.

'Yes. For me there is only one supreme God or Power or Source of all creation – call it what you will. To become entrenched in the detail of sectarian rules just complicates that simple fact. I am as at home in a Jewish synagogue as in a mosque or a cathedral or a village chapel. Surely, it's the same God for all, is it not?'

'That's a very easy way out of commitment to a religious discipline,' she replied. 'Anyway, my husband has no God of any kind, so what do I do with that?'

'That's not true,' I said. 'He has a God, all right. He just doesn't know it,' I suggested. 'God does not depart merely because your husband doesn't believe. Why not ask him to describe the kind of God there might be if he was to believe in one? You might be surprised at his answer.'

We left it at that and shortly after I was invited to her home for dinner – so I could 'chat' to her husband.

'Hold on,' I said, 'I am a divorce lawyer not a preacher!'

It seems the case that many young people who marry take little heed of their religious beliefs beforehand as they are preoccupied with more romantic and practical matters. If both parties have had an upbringing where a basic Christian belief is taken for granted, although perhaps not practised in church, the happy couple simply trundle on in the same vein using the church when needed: to marry, to visit occasionally and for subsequent events with a religious connotation, such as christenings. Possibly this tendency is more prevalent for marriages with a Christian background than for, say, Jewish or Islamic marriages when, in many instances, the religious element in the relationship and in marriage is taken more seriously. Having said that, it does appear the case that the 'middle ground' of all the major religions practised in the Western world breeds a relaxed and non-demanding religious culture with social, family and business values taking priority. This view is, of course, somewhat limited to my first-hand experiences in England. I realise there are significant differences in the Middle East and beyond.

Differing religious doctrines enrich our understanding of life and the world about us. However, when one or more sectarian groups seek to impose their beliefs on others, conflict and offence is caused. This can also be the case in marriage. When spouses are at odds with each other over religious differences a lack of tolerance and acceptance may be revealed in the relationship, which, ironically, exposes just how lacking the husband or wife or both are in true religious belief and understanding.

Consequently, it is a wise move to open up the subject of religion in meaningful discussion when talking of marriage. At least cover the basics of each other's religious beliefs, if any, and whether either of you feel strongly about any particular religious principles, which may affect your daily lives together. The venue for the marriage, if in a religious setting, will in many cases be the starting point for such discussion. After your wedding do you both wish to attend church services regularly? If you have children is there a specific faith you prefer for them? Is there a preference for a particular denomination for schooling? Do you wish your children to undergo a religious initiation?

Religion may not be top priority on the wedding day, but it may become so later on in married life. Be prepared.

I recall one husband coming to see me who had married a Mormon. He explained that he had married her because she would not sleep with him outside of wedlock. Otherwise, he would have preferred for them just to live together for a while before taking the plunge. Two years on, he was feeling the pinch of being called to account for his shortcomings of not embracing the Mormon faith.

'You know, when Marion agreed to marry me she knew I was being driven by my sexual desire for her. Marion said it did not matter because she believed in Paul's teachings in the New Testament, that it is better for a man to take a wife than to become a fornicator. It is better for a man to contain himself for his wife than to wander into a sexual abyss. If he cannot be celibate, a wife is the next best option. So, in a way, Marion thought she was saving me from damnation. I went along with her reasoning because it suited me, but now things have moved on.'

Appetite again, I thought. 'Do you have children?' I asked.

'No, and there lies the rub. Marion will not have children until our marriage is sealed in the temple. She says that our marriage is so far only an earthly marriage because we were married before the registrar. I would have had to convert to be married in the temple. To be fair, Marion did not ask me to convert and I never mentioned the subject.'

'So, tell me how things change if you marry in a temple,' I enquired. Frankly, I knew little about the Mormon marriage rules, only having encountered an introduction to the faith on my front doorstep from time to time when young missionaries visited. On one occasion, I recall inviting them in to show me a short film explaining their basic beliefs; the most memorable to me being that Christ will come again and be ruler of the world.

'Things change dramatically,' my concerned client explained, answering my question. 'When a marriage is sealed in the temple it becomes everlasting beyond death. It becomes eternal. Marion feels that the strength a temple marriage will bring to our relationship will be the rock upon which to build our family life.'

'Does Marion consider an earthly marriage to be second best, then?'

'Yes, she does, but you know she has done me a service because I never gave religion a thought before I met Marion. I was quite happy to remain a simple non-practising Protestant. Marriage to me was about love and passion, not religion.'

'Don't you think religion is about love and passion?' I asked.

'I do now,' he replied. 'Now I realise I have beliefs of

my own, which do not include a number of the Mormon doctrines. Actually, I believe that too many religious rules made by man, however well-intentioned, are a poor substitute for the real thing. One might know all the rules backwards and live by the letter of them, but know nothing of God in a true and real sense. People who are truly religious simply practice love without charge, favour or demand. My children will be no more loved and cherished because of a temple marriage than a makeshift marriage on a desert island.'

'So, what do you require from me?' I asked. 'Surely, you believe in respecting another person's religious beliefs, including Marion's. After all, you married her knowing she believed strongly in her Mormon faith,' I said. 'If you love her enough can you not come to terms with it and accept a temple marriage?'

'No. I've explained already. I would have to convert. I am not prepared to do it,' he replied.

'But if your belief is simply that love conquers all, what do the rules matter? Will you not prosper anyway in your love regardless of the rules?'

'I did not say love conquers all. In fact, love does not conquer. It is long suffering of others who have not found its healing ways. I said that practising love is the only true religion. If I convert and we have children they will have to be brought up in the Mormon faith.'

'What's wrong with that?' I said. 'If love is long suffering then suffer Marion as good practice for your love,' I added, albeit with a smile.

'No!' he declared. 'I do not believe in many of their teachings and I do not wish my children to be indoctrinated with them. They need to remain free enough to choose how they approach religion when they are old enough to discover it for themselves. I believe it's inside us all along from the beginning, or even before, sleeping, as it were, until it's time to awaken.'

'Would the children not discover their religion anyway? Could indoctrination not serve to awaken them when their inner feelings rise up in protest?' I asked. 'On the other hand, they may embrace the Mormon faith and enrich it with their own feelings for God and love. You cannot lose surely. At least they would have a structure and order to their religious upbringing, which provides a moral code for them in these wayward times.' I could tell he was becoming frustrated with our discussion.

'I'm sorry, but I want a divorce,' he said firmly. 'I know how I feel and Marion is not for me eternally. There will be no temple marriage.'

That was the end of it. The man got his divorce. I heard later that he had converted to Catholicism.

11

Conclusions

In this book I have endeavoured to address the basic elements of human nature, which, from the perspective of a divorce lawyer, have featured in my work. Most of us can relate to our appetite and its excesses. Equally, the quality of love in our lives, or the apparent lack of it, needs no introduction. Perhaps it is not so easy to accept the idea of gender differences and the need to 'marry up' the male and female energies that function within us, so there is an improved harmony of being. However, marriage is made within the individual and, whether or not married on the 'outside' with another, this 'first' marriage is paramount. The external marriage between husband and wife is the greatest relational aid towards attaining this self-fulfilled state of being.

There is a direct link between the self development of one's own internal state and the development of one's 'worldly' marriage. Improve your relational qualities with your partner and you inevitably improve yourself. If, as a husband, you curb your male ego excesses and practice a sensitive approach to your wife's needs you gain greater internal balance. If, as a wife, you refrain from reactive emotional displays and seek a more balanced response to your relational problems you will achieve greater self-control.

This may be a rarefied concept to accept, but ultimately I believe each of us is destined for self-fulfilment and enlightenment. A helpmate along the way makes all the difference to the journey.

And for the journey it is useful for all of us to realise at least some of the potential pitfalls. Mistakes and difficulties will visit most marriages. If affirmed and tackled positively they become stepping stones to wisdom. So, this book is not about avoiding such encounters, but rather, hopefully, being a little better prepared to handle them. Whether there is an issue concerning finance, children, emotions, sex, religion or just unpalatable opposition, it is helpful to have some insight into the snakes that hide amidst the jungle of marital life.

Yet, above all, remember and practice love. Find it if you feel you have not got it operating in your daily life. In Marion's story, you might recall that her husband said love does not seek to conquer and that it is long suffering. It can afford to be long suffering, for there is nothing other than love when all is said and done. Only the clouds of earthly living blank it out for a time. Ultimately, we shall all bathe in its light again. Love does not need to conquer, for it has always been ever-present, and it is merely mankind's ignorance which has denied it.

I wish you well on your journey.